ATE DUE

# Dutch architecture after 1900

R. BLIJSTRA

# Dutch architecture after 1900

With forty photographs and a list of buildings completed since 1945

P. N. van Kampen & Zoon N.V. - Amsterdam

A country's architecture is largely determined by its size, its climate, its geographical position and its physical features.

The Netherlands is modest in size, its climate is temperate, it is surrounded by a number of large countries and it has the physical characteristics of a delta region, a clay mass once covered by the sea.

In view of the modest size of the country, the Netherlands can boast few really large buildings; no mighty kings or princes of the Church built their palaces, cathedrals, castles or monasteries there. It is to the burgher's initiative that the Netherlands owes its finest buildings, and the most noteworthy examples of its architecture before 1900 are therefore mainly town halls and private dwellings in towns both large and small.

It is those town halls, the unobtrusive churches and the rows of houses of the well-to-do lining the canals that give the Dutch towns their special charm: not a blatant charm but one that has to be discovered.

The temperate climate of the Netherlands calls for a special building style, one that lets in the sun and yet gives proper protection against the cold, with large but well-fitting windows.

It is just as well to stress this point, since warning voices are occasionally heard from various quarters against the current trend of admitting plenty of light into dwellings, offices and workplaces by the free use of glass. Those same voices go on to point out that this is an international phenomenon, forgetting that the Dutch have always preferred light and air to a dark and musty atmosphere.

The fact that the Netherlands is hemmed about by a number of large countries and has intensive traffic also with distant territories has encouraged an exchange of cultures. The Netherlands has never been afraid of outside influences, it has never sought to isolate itself; and in architecture it has copied all the European styles, adapting them, however, to its own character, which has been determined not only by its climate and size but also by its physical features.

A special characteristic of the country is that the land has been wrested from the sea and is consequently looked upon as a treasured possession. The Dutch abhor waste of land and, in consequence, also waste of space; they therefore prefer to build in a compact and economical fashion. Another factor determining Dutch architecture, also attributable to the country's physical features, is the lack of natural stone. Clay, baked into bricks, is the building material the Dutch have had to rely on. By the very nature of their manufacturing process, bricks are small in size, a fact likely to encourage attention to detail.

From the above-mentioned factors, which have played an important part in determining Dutch architecture, we can make out certain frequently recurring fundamental characteristics, viz. the fact that Dutch architects are not out to design imposing buildings and that they are suspicious of the monumental. The Dutch like openness and this manifests itself, curiously enough, in the practice people have, in the towns, of not drawing their curtains at night; they are susceptible to outside influences; they abhor waste of space and they love detail. These fundamental principles should be borne in mind when one examines the development of Dutch architecture during the first half of the twentieth century.

6

Those who have no first-hand knowledge of the Netherlands and who have not studied its history do not always understand the sharp division in Dutch society on denominational lines. The Dutch are quick to perceive the mentality and religion of those they meet and will adjust their conduct according as they have to deal with persons of their own faith or those of other persuasions. In politics and in social life, as also in artistic and intellectual spheres, there is a clear distinction between Roman Catholics, Protestants – who in turn are split up into different sects – and humanists. This distinction is particularly noticeable when the Dutch pass judgment on their compatriots. They are more tolerant towards people from other countries. This peculiar characteristic of the Dutch explains their hospitality and the fair measure of open-heartedness they display towards foreigners; also their readiness to give careful study to foreign thoughts and ideas, without necessarily adopting them immediately. But once they have become rooted in the minds of one section of the public, it will often happen that another section will oppose them.

The aversion to the monumental and to waste of space (to put it positively, the great attention given to the planned use of ground) and the love of detail in the traditional sense also influence those who wish to depart from the traditional, for the latter, too, display these typically Dutch qualities. Openness is a question frequently discussed in the Netherlands now that, throughout the world, there is a trend to build in a more 'open' fashion; opposition to 'internationalism' carried too far has something to do with this.

The struggle between internationalism (those opposing it equate it with uniformity, plagiarism, renunciation of one's true character) and national style constitutes a fascinating chapter in the history of modern Dutch architecture, though the debates on the subject are not always of equal interest. The history of the use of new materials and construction methods, which had already been devised and partly developed in the nineteenth century but not adopted to any extent until the twentieth century, runs parallel with this struggle and is closely connected with it. That is why foreign building trends and building techniques, often first perfected abroad, must have our attention. Indeed, foreign influence and building techniques are regular subjects of discussion among present day Dutch architects.

In the Netherlands, too, especially since 1945, building projects have been conceived on a considerably larger scale. This fact is manifest, especially in the expansion plans of large towns, in the high blocks of flats being erected, in the new motorways, but more than anything else in the extensive hydraulic engineering works in the centre and south-west of the country and in the harbour building on the Rhine delta. Nevertheless, this 'scaling-up' has not spoilt the country's rural aspect, although it is seriously endangered in the west, in the 'Randstad', the West Holland conurbation formed by the towns of Amsterdam, Haarlem, Leyden, The Hague, Delft, Rotterdam, Gouda, Utrecht and Hilversum, partly because of indiscriminate building here and there in the 'green heart' of this ring.

Sketching a summary yet true general picture of the development of Dutch architecture during the last century in so far as it followed more or less a course of its own, or fitted in, more or less, with international trends, one can make out three distinct periods. It would be true to say that in the latter half of the nineteenth century Dutch architecture depended almost entirely on foreign influence and its own past; it began to break away from that influence in the beginning of this century and, in the nineteen thirties, it tried to find its own form, without, however, ignoring what was happening in other countries. Although it is true that, after the last examples of Dutch classicism, new buildings of some architectural interest were constructed in the first half of the nineteenth century, eclecticism, the imitation of old styles, predominated to such an extent that it can hardly be said that Dutch architecture possessed a style of its own. A few good buildings were indeed put up in imitation Gothic, imitation Renaissance and imitation Baroque, but they might just as well have been built elsewhere. Eclecticism was then truly international.

In some ways Dr. M. P. J. Cuypers can be regarded as the architect who initiated the change. True enough, he was following closely in the footsteps of Viollet le Duc, but at the same time he tried to introduce Dutch elements, notably those of the Dutch Renaissance.

Then came Berlage, at first also an eclectic. The surprising development of this remarkable pioneer, whose intellect overshadowed his aesthetic insight, can be clearly traced in his Amsterdam Exchange building. From his original plans of 1885 – for a building in Dutch Renaissance style – he proceeded through a number of modified drafts to the final creation, which possibly still shows, in parts, romanesque-romantic traits, but which in spirit is far removed from all 'examples'. The Exchange thus marks a new epoch in Dutch architecture, even though it embodies a few typically non-Dutch features, with its monumental and 'closed-in' aspects.

In those days there were several architects who, either more or less independently or working together, sought to banish eclecticism: Garnier and Perret in France, Frank Lloyd Wright in America, Voysey in England, Olbrich, Loos, Wagner and Behrens in Germany and Austria, Horta in Belgium, and Gaudi in Spain. Some of these architects could be classified among the exponents of 'Art Nouveau', 'Jugendstil', later also called Macaroni or Whiplash style; but Berlage did not belong to this group. Around 1900 it seems as if all these architects, working alone or in groups, some a little wildly, others more cautiously, were all consciously endeavouring to create a new style.

Berlage certainly did not lag behind these pioneers. His work around 1900 shows little sign of being influenced by the trends in other countries. Traces of the 'Jugendstil' or 'Art Nouveau' are, however, to be found in his designs of furniture and in a number of architectural details such as the porches of the office building of the insurance company 'De Nederlanden' in Muntplein in Amsterdam (1895).

The 'Jugendstil', of which the first clear example was the house at No. 12, rue de Turin (now the rue Emile Jackson) in Brussels, designed in 1893 by Horta, made a clean break with eclecticism, but in later years was widely regarded with scorn. It is often forgotten, however, that the 'Jugendstil' was at first also of significance in the field of architecture and that its innovations were not, originally, confined to the wild ornamentation that later excited ridicule. Especially in Germany and Austria, the 'Jugendstil' degenerated into a purely ornamental and superficial symbolism, but in the Netherlands, where the proper limits of architectural art were more instinctively apprehended, buildings arose to which later generations have not done full justice, for instance, a number of large clothing stores, the house at 42, Denneweg in The Hague, the railway station at Haarlem, the premises of the Utrecht Life Assurance Company, etc. Buildings in the style of the 'Art Nouveau' or 'Jugendstil' are frequently occupied by companies that began to flourish at the end of the nineteenth century and early in the twentieth century, such as newspaper printing works, pharmacies, etc. Examples of the 'Art Nouveau' are to be found in the Netherlands particularly in places that became popular in the beginning of the twentieth century as holiday resorts (Scheveningen, Apeldoorn), as shopping centres for the well-to-do (Utrecht, The Hague), or as regional centres (Tilburg, Meppel, Breda), the style being most pronounced, of course, in places near the Belgian border; in fact, 'Art Nouveau' was at first sometimes referred to in the Netherlands as the Belgian style. It is a curious fact, though quite logical really, that within towns examples of 'Art Nouveau' are most often to be found in the neighbourhood of railway stations, especially between the station and the town centre. The Dutch 'Art Nouveau' was, however, a rather restrained version of the building styles prevalent at that period in other countries. This period, which has long been out of favour, is now regaining popularity to some extent, although unlike elsewhere imitation of the style is being carefully eschewed in the Netherlands. It is worthy of note – and this does not speak well for the vitality of this style – that the architects who adopted it remained quite unknown, which clearly shows that they were unable to hold their own at a time when other demands were being made. The style lent itself to imitation by incompetent architects, who adopted forms for which they had neither feeling nor understanding.

The demands of the period soon became clear once Berlage had given the impetus to an entirely new building style, an impetus so strong that its influence was still felt in many respects far into the twentieth century. The development of Dutch architecture can best be understood if Berlage is regarded as the father of this architecture, but a father who had not only obedient but also recalcitrant and obstinate children. For an architect's influence resembles any other cultural development in so far as the latest stage of a trend is seldom taken as the starting-point for new activity: later generations usually seize upon some aspect typifying the middle period of an artist's work to emulate and develop.

This is not true in the case of slavish imitators, but Berlage did not have any, could not have any, for his work was so broad in its range and his principles afforded so many possibilities. It is significant that Berlage was a socialist at a time when this political conviction had, in the Netherlands, a distinctly romantic flavour, and that his keenest disciple, Kropholler, was one of the leading Roman Catholic architects: a remarkable exception to the rule that in the Netherlands the artistic sphere is divided according to intellectual, even religious, principles. Kropholler is especially well known for the town halls he built in medium-sized and small municipalities (many being near The Hague), but much of the style originated by Berlage is also to be found in his churches. This style is characterized by its honest and even profuse use of bricks, by a certain affinity with the romanesque, by the attention lavished on detail and fondness for the architectural art, by clear-cut lines of construction, and by the use of natural stone in a manner that shows that Berlage, too, was not always simply the servant of construction, but clearly strove to create his own style. In addition to Kropholler, De Bazel and Hanrath can also be considered the successors of Berlage – successors, not imitators. Kromhout is a sort of go-between who, influenced initially by 'Art Nouveau', passed by way of Berlage into a different camp. Oud, Dudok, and Staal originally belonged to the Berlage School too, but they later went their separate ways.

Four dates are the landmarks in respect of the four other movements. In 1912 the 'Scheepvaarthuis' (Shipping Office) was built in Amsterdam; it was the first important work of the Amsterdam School. In 1916 the garden village of Vreewijk was designed by Granpré Molière, who later inspired the Delft School. 1917 saw the first publication of 'De Stijl' (The Style), a magazine on which the architects J. J. P. Oud, C. van Eesteren and G. T. Rietveld collaborated. In 1927 the group called 'The Eight' published its manifesto; later it joined the C.I.A.M. Congrès Internationaux d'Architecture Moderne.

It is rather difficult to draw the dividing lines between the different architectural movements in the Netherlands and it is true to say that before World War II they were in a continual state of flux. However, a closer study does reveal a definite pattern. Berlage should be seen as a man who lived in a period of transition in architecture, a period which he himself helped to create. His activity in the field of architectural thought had many facets. He fought eclecticism, he advocated 'honesty' in constructional design and in the use of materials; he was against camouflaging them. He accepted the newly invented materials, such as reinforced concrete, but at the same time he had a great esteem for sound craftsmanship and attention to detail.

If we lay the emphasis on Berlage's preference for 'honesty' in construction and his acceptance of new materials, we can look upon him as the precursor of the 'Stijl' group, which in its architectural conceptions was in turn the precursor of the 'The Eight' group, the group of moderns that later joined the C.I.A.M.

If we consider in the first place the pure craftsmanship and the Dutch spirit of his work, we associate him with the Delft School, which, however, was to pay more attention to the romance of history than Berlage did. The Amsterdam School, on the other hand, does not seem to have been fathered by Berlage; it is rather the antithesis of the Berlage School. In some respects this is very true, for the Amsterdam School was to some extent a reaction against the simplicity and starkness of his designs, which often resulted in a harsh effect. If, however, we look upon Berlage as the first architect in the Netherlands to replace eclecticism by new forms, the Amsterdam School may be considered to have carried on his work.

But Berlage was not alone in his opposition to eclecticism; 'originality' was now all the rage and was carried to such lengths as to become almost absurd, purely outward form becoming the all-important factor in architecture.

If some of the architects already mentioned can be considered Berlage's obedient children, the adherents of the Amsterdam School may be looked upon as wayward children who turned against their father. Berlage was generally acknowledged to have been the first to consciously oppose the imitation of style prevalent in the nineteenth century, but it was felt that he had not gone far enough. The younger architects also thought that, though Berlage had had a purifying influence on architecture, he had, for one thing, used concrete in a manner inconsonant with its true nature.

However, one should not imagine that the younger men were themselves more competent in their use of concrete. The truth was quite otherwise. The Amsterdam School's first effort was a building, the 'Scheepvaarthuis' in Amsterdam (1911–1915), whose concrete framework was encased in draperies of brickwork and sculptures, the adherents of this school using the bricks rather as mouldings than as brickwork.

It is interesting here to note that De Klerk, in a remarkable enquiry held among his colleagues in 1916 into Berlage's significance in architecture, made the curious observation: 'In my opinion, Berlage ceased to be representative some ten years ago. The sparkling novelty, the sensationally startling and impressive features with which present-day technology regularly surprises us and which characterize the really modern style, is not felt by him – at all events, he has never given us any reason to believe that he does feel these things. It had been expected that Berlage would excel, for instance, in ferro-concrete construction (i.e. reinforced concrete), but he has used that brand-new material in a manner quite out of keeping with its nature, hiding it away as an auxiliary material in exactly the same way as all the other Dutch architects have done. Summarizing, Berlage has undoubtedly done a great service to architecture in so far as he has purified it, but he has been unable to exercise any influence on architectural style. His field of activity was too confined, it was too exclusively technical and utilitarian to have any cultural significance'.

The reproach was unfair; De Klerk was making the same mistake as many other young people make when trying at all costs to prove themselves different from older generations. If he had studied, objectively, a lecture given by Berlage in the winter of 1907–1908, he would have realized that Berlage's point of view was not so very different from his own. On that occasion Berlage had said: 'The architect of today is faced with the same problem as of old, namely, to create space with new and well-tried materials, but in particular with such materials as give satisfaction to people today; and, since developments in that direction are now also showing a businesslike trend, the aim is to create space covered by large roofs with few supports. Since it is man's constant endeavour to give substance to his ideals in the constructions he creates, the architect can, indeed he must, use more materials than before if he is to meet the needs of our times and satisfy the demands of utility. He will even be obliged to use ferro-concrete, not only for roofing, but for the entire construction, if it becomes clear that utility requires it; he will have to make use of plateglass windows, basically for the same reason as an engineer uses asphalt in road-making. But it is also his task and his duty to see that these materials are used in such a way that, like nature itself, he provides for more than pure utility'.

Both De Klerk and Berlage, then, accepted reinforced concrete as a worthy building material. However, De Klerk was critical of Berlage's use of reinforced concrete, alleging that he employed it in a manner inconsonant with its true nature. The strange thing is that De Klerk himself, together with his Amsterdam School, used materials of every kind, even bricks, those thrusty old friends – which they employed either by choise or necessity – in ways that, while testifying to the architects, great virtuosity, were hardly in keeping with the materials' distinctive character. So opposition to Berlage's ideas did not stem from a difference in views in the technical field but rather from a difference in the conception of design.

In the eyes of the younger generation Berlage was too dry, too much of the sober Dutchman. The sting of De Klerk's criticism lay in the tail: 'His field of activity was too narrowly confined; it was too exclusively technical and utilitarian to have any cultural value'. Berlage was anything but a visionary, and imagination was a first essential in the Amsterdam School. One need only note the excited tone of an article in 'Wendingen', the periodical truly representative of these younger men: 'Begone, all of you who wish to stipulate the way in which your house shall be built! For the artist, you do not exist. You whom he detests, you who supply him with the money, but obstruct him with your demands, you who give instructions that cramp his style. Roaming hordes of unorganized forces are about again, moving exultantly from place to place, full of enthusiasm, like the Nomads of the desert, leaving the smoking ruins of the houses of cards in their wake – those debilitated efforts from a period of materialism – the four walls and a roof. They are miscreants and flamethrowers in society, they openly destroy the laboriously built-up system of architectural design and set fire to huge heaps of T-squares and set squares, bevels and rulers. Dancing like satyrs around the glowing and smoking mass, they sing a song of liberation and enlightenment. Away with those façades that so clearly determined the front, the back and the side of a building so that those who took themselves for architects designed façades instead of living space'.

It is hard to say exactly what provoked this passionate outburst. To some extent, the Amsterdam School showed traces of a late blossoming of 'Art Nouveau', the impact of which had not been great in the Netherlands, so that it had perhaps not entirely eradicated eclecticism; or it may have been opposition to Berlage, who was too austere; or the influence of expressionism, though certainly not the German expressionism of Hans Poelzig or Otto Bartning with their 'Grosses Schauspiel' or the 'Sternkirche', but rather that of Mendelsohn; perhaps it was Frank Lloyd Wright's influence (yet this is doubtful; a country house of his was copied almost exactly in 1915 by Robert van 't Hoff at Huis ter Heide, even though this architect, who later designed hardly anything, was considered to belong to the 'De Stijl' group). Certainly the East Asian – Indonesian – forms exerted considerable influence. All this made for a notable individual style, lively enough, but first and foremost decorative, despite the fact that the older architects were accused of designing façades rather than living space.

The tragedy of the Amsterdam School was the fact that it was merely given an opportunity to design façades. After the First World War, Amsterdam Municipality made it a requirement that the façades of privately built blocks of houses and flats should be designed by architects. This resulted in the appearance of the often fantastic façades of the Southern and Western districts of Amsterdam, which for some time impressed not only the Dutch but also many foreigners by reason of their daring design. The layout of the dwellings themselves, however, showed no changes, so that in fact no real progress was made; in professional circles this building style often was referred to as 'schortjesarchitectuur' (apron architecture). Yet, it is understandable that people should have a soft spot for those buildings, if only because the Dutch, who abroad had always had the reputation of being too austere and lacking in imagination, had thereby shown that they could sometimes be wild and unrestrained. Despite the intense individualism, which concerned itself but little with the requirements of the contemporary society, it has been a glorious period in Dutch architecture, even though the excesses did become unbearable after a little while and the details, like those of 'Art Nouveau', lent themselves too readily to imitation. The Amsterdam style was soon represented by a collection of frontispieces, designed by clever people, behind which they concealed their bad lay-outs. And the same was true of their country houses, where they did, after all, have a freer hand. Even De Klerk, the most talented of these architects, could not break free from this duplicity. Because he needed massive elements with which to front the street, he combined six apartment houses in the Henriette Ronnerplein (1921) into one unit that looks like a super-country house. It is consequently a monumental affair, a construction that gives no inkling that its function is to house ordinary people.

To understand properly the importance of this new movement in design, one should realize that the opposition to eclecticism, which had not yet been completely ousted in the Netherlands, was very great indeed. Its general influence, which made itself felt also in the arts and crafts and in the art of poster designing, was much greater than is often realized today. It was particularly in those years that a great deal of interest was shown abroad in Dutch architecture. After Berlage this interest was maintained, opening the way, as it were, for the subsequent, most glorious period of the functionalists and the members of the 'De Stijl' group. Nor should one overlook the fact that members of the Amsterdam School were consistent in their treatment of the housefronts along the streets, as had already been recommended by Berlage, for they gave more heed to breaking new ground than to the risk that, by fanciful use of brick, they might end up adopting a sort of 'art for art's sake' attitude.

With De Klerk's death in 1923, this exaggerated opposition to eclecticism in a country that had not experienced the equally strange 'Art Nouveau' as an intensive catharsis in its architecture (as it had in its painting, printing and arts and crafts) lost its leader and ablest representative. Nevertheless, the Amsterdam School continued, even after 1920, to be an important movement in Dutch architecture and brought much influence to bear, not only in the field of architecture, through the medium of its periodical 'Wendingen'. Talented representatives were Kramer, Van der Mey, Wijdeveld, Buys, Greiner, Wils, who later joined the 'De Stijl', group, and Mertens. Others connected with the movement were H. A. J. and Jan Baanders, J. Crouwel, Co Brandes, P. Vorkink, C. J. Blaauw, and J. G. Schelling, who in his designs of railway stations followed –

albeit at a distance – several different movements. At first, both W. Dudok, and J. F. Staal, originally followers of Berlage, were also members of this school, but the former became an individualist with his well-known block formation, which I should hesitate to call cubistic, whereas the latter turned more and more towards functionalism. Kromhout started as an exponent of 'Art Nouveau', later came under Berlage's influence, and finally became a representative of the Amsterdam School.

It is possible to trace the development of external design, beginning with Berlage and continuing far into the twentieth century (Berlage's design of the Christian Science Church in The Hague (1925) is not entirely free from the influence of the Amsterdam School, the movement that had so vigorously opposed him!) right up to 1930 and, in actual fact, until the beginning of World War II. It runs parallel to the development of architecture proper, in which construction, function and design are indissolubly united, from Berlage's time to the present day. It should be remembered that Berlage was a pioneer not only in the work he produced but also in his ideas, pointing out as early as 1907–1908 that construction should be executed in simple forms and that the new materials should be accepted, with the proviso, of course, that the architect should take account of their usefulness and hence their function: like nature, he should be attentive to more than usefulness and function when using them in his designs. We have seen that the Amsterdam School, which got bogged down in designs that were too fantastic, at first accused Berlage of using new materials in a manner foreign to their nature, so it is true to say that Berlage's principles were adopted even though his examples were not approved of, and though a different path – that of free fantasy – was taken later on.

However, the development can be traced fairly clearly through to J. J. P. Oud, who, while Berlage was the father of Dutch architecture, can justifiably be called its conscience.

With the appearance of Oud, we have now come to the famous 'De Stijl' group, better known abroad nowadays than the once famous Amsterdam School. At about the same time and, in many respects, on surprisingly parallel lines, the 'Bauhaus' movement was initiated in Germany under the leadership of Gropius. The exact relationship between the 'De Stijl' group (named after the magazine of that name, 1917–1931) and the 'Bauhaus', which started at Dessau and later moved to Weimar, needs further investigation. It is a fact, however, that the founder of the 'De Stijl' group, Theo van Doesburg, gave lectures to the pupils of the Bauhaus which most certainly influenced the development of that movement. However, it is probably more a case of interchange of ideas than of influence being exerted exclusively from one side.

According to Oud, Gropius built a house at Lichtervelde as late as 1920–1921 that can be looked upon as a log cabin richly decorated with wood-carvings. In 1922, however, when designing the theatre at Jena, he suddenly went over to stark, white, angular and simple architecture. This switch to the abstract was so abrupt and so striking that it may safely be ascribed to Van Doesburg's influence and his exposition of 'De Stijl' theories. Rietveld's 'board' furniture too, for that matter, has clearly left its mark on certain types of 'Bauhaus' furniture. The book on Mies van der Rohe's work written by Philip Johnson and published by the Museum of Modern Art in New York reveals that Mies van der Rohe too, was influenced by 'De Stijl' in 1923. Oud further maintains that even the work of Le Corbusier shows occasional traces of 'De Stijl'. It should, however, be stated that originality for its own sake in architecture is not a merit. Moreover, 'De Stijl' itself must have derived from something, though there is no point in trying to trace at all costs its origins and bring them under the heading of any particular trend or movement; any new movement must needs have many sources and sometimes it is quite impossible to trace them.

To understand properly the 'De Stijl' movement, one should appreciate that it would be incorrect to say that the 'De Stijl' group was originally more pictorial-cubistic (as opposed to the Amsterdam School, which might then be called pictorial-expressionistic) than architecturally oriented. One can more rightly term the work of Dudok and Buys pictorial-cubistic, as perhaps also the work of some other members of the Amsterdam School, whereas 'De Stijl' had, perhaps, in its origin close ties with the plastic arts; but they were not so strong that the architects belonging to the movement allowed themselves to be overwhelmed by them. Although Mondriaan and Van Doesburg set the tone of the movement's magazine, a tone that now sounds too shrill and unintelligible in our ears, the architects showed from the very start that they were well able to get seriously to grips with the problems of modern times. Mondriaan, who is at present enthusiastically hailed by the non-figurative painters as the most important member of the 'De Stijl' group, had nothing to do with the architecture of that time, except perhaps in his use of colour. A revival of Mondriaan's colours, which are sometimes adopted by certain Dutch architects without any rhyme or reason, does not signify a revival of the architectural ideas of the 'De Stijl' group. Such a revival would, in fact, be impossible in view of the new building techniques and materials evolved in the last thirty years.

To discover the architectural principles of the 'De Stijl' group, we should examine the work of Oud, who began by producing a few designs in the style of the 'De Stijl' group. In his ideas, however, he followed in the footsteps of Berlage, though taking a somewhat divergent course.

In its first year of publication Oud wrote in the 'De Stijl' magazine: 'The development of architecture is not determined only by intellectual but also largely by social and technical influences, for architecture, more than any other form of art, is rooted in social life and even in its most individual expression remains bound by social considerations'. And a little further on he writes: 'Architecture might well be termed an indirect form of art, since the idealism of art must find expression by way of utility. If utility were subordinated to idealism, it would be at the expense of general and cultural values, and such would not be conducive to the creation of a sound style. It is therefore of greater importance, where development of architectural style is concerned, that a house be good (i.e. pure, in the technical and practical sense) than beautiful. On this basis alone can one consciously aim at a good style. The emergence of a style at any one period is so much the result of various jointly acting influences that it is impossible to give a likely explanation of the phenomenon. What can be categorically affirmed, however, is the fact that its form will not be based on the outward forms of older styles, but that it will be rooted in the substance of contemporary techniques and society, as has always been the case, with the result that it will have a completely different character from that of an earlier style period. It is therefore essential that modern architects should, first and foremost, be thoroughly trained technicians (or at least have a thorough understanding of modern building techniques) and that they be fully conversant with social conditions in the broadest sense.

If we compare the pronouncements of Berlage and Oud, it at once becomes apparent that there is a distinct difference in their basic characters (Berlage, the orthodox pioneer, laying emphasis on the fact that architecture must take account of more than considerations of utility; Oud, essentially sophisticated, yet stressing utility as a factor which should not be subservient to any other), but we can also see that ideas were changing in accordance with the development of architecture in that period. There was never any doubt in Berlage's mind that architecture must be an art; Oud, who had already dissociated himself from the Amsterdam School, was rather suspicious of that word 'art' and made utility an integral part of the conception of architecture. This clearly shows that, although he wrote for the 'De Stijl' magazine, he was not in agreement with the group's manifestos, from which he withheld his signature. The architects connected with the magazine 'De Stijl', which ceased publication when Theo van Doesburg died in 1931, pursued ideals that differed somewhat from those of the painters with whom they collaborated.

Oud once again clearly formulated the then current point of view of the architects in his book 'Mein Weg in "De Stijl"'. On page 13 he wrote: 'No more little masterpieces for the individual, no more exquisite mansions with fine touches of handicraft and luxurious decoration, but mass production and standardization with a view to providing decent dwellings for the masses. Detail for detail's sake was to be abandoned in the interests of the whole. Machine-produced components were to be accepted on their own merits, and no longer in substitution or imitation of handicraft. The precision which we admired in purely mechanical products, such as motor-cars, steamships, instruments, etc., was to provide the foundation for a complete reappraisal of architecture. Henceforth, the requirements which a building had to satisfy were to be determined with equal precision and realized with the latest materials, constructional forms and working methods. The aim was to be a better use of space, more practical kitchens, more attention to the position of a dwelling in relation to the sun, etc. In other words, an endeavour was made to achieve the optimum result in a small space by rationalization and standardization. A house à la Ford, all light, air and colour.'

Van Doesburg, the remarkable, very individualistic, very strong 'mediator', largely agreed with this, as evidenced by his article in 'De Stijl', volume VI, pages 78 to 82 entitled 'Tot een beeldende architectuur' (Towards a Plastic Form of Architecture); we here quote a number of essential points which figure on page 32 of catalogue 81 published by the 'Stedelijk Museum' of Amsterdam.

1. The form. The essential condition for a sound development of architecture (and of art in general) is the discarding of all preconceived conceptions of form. Instead of using former style types as patterns and thus copying former styles, the problem of architecture has to be approached from an entirely new angle.

2. The new form of architecture is elemental, in other words, it is developed from the basic principles of building in the broadest sense. These elemental principles, including function, mass, plane, time, space, light, colour, material, etc., are at the same time plastic elements.

3. The new form of architecture is economical, in other words, it organizes its basic means in as businesslike and economical a manner as possible, neither overlooking means nor wasting material.

4. The new form of architecture is functional, in other words, it is developed from an accurate evaluation of practical requirements, which are embodied in a clear fundamental plan.

5. The new architecture has no form and yet it is determinate, in other words, it does not recognize any preconceived scheme of aesthetic forms; no forms into which it pours, like pastry cooks, the functional spaces deriving from the practical demands of housing.

Unlike all former styles, the new architectural method does not carry within itself any narrowly defined type or basic form. The arrangement of an area in functional spaces is strictly determined by rectangular planes that have no inherent individual forms because, although limited (one plane by the other), they can be extended ad infinitum, thereby creating a co-ordinate system of which the various points correspond with an equal number of points in space. This means that a direct relationship arises between the planes and the (outer) open space.

6. The new form of architecture has released the concept of the monumental

dimensional relationship.

14. The colour. The new form of architecture has put an end to the art of painting as a separate, imaginative expression of harmony, be it secondarily by means of images or primarily by means of coloured planes. The new form of architecture incorporates colour as a direct element of expression of its proportions in time and space. Without colour those proportions would fail to come alive, they would pass unnoticed.

It is colour that brings out the well-balanced lines and forms of architectural proportions. To organize them into a harmonious whole (not into a single plane, not into two dimensions, but into the new conception of four-dimensional space time) is the task of modern painters.

At a further stage of development this colour could be replaced by denaturalized material having a colour of its own (a task for the chemists); but only where such a material is required for practical reasons.

15. The new form of architecture is anti-decorative. Those who are shy of using colour should realize that colour is not merely decorative or ornamental, but has become an element of expression inherent in modern architecture.

16. Architecture as the synthesis of the new plasticism. The art of building is a part of the new form of architecture, taking for its substance a compound of all the arts in their most elemental forms. It posits the possibility of thinking in terms of four dimensions; in other words, the 'plastic' architects, among whom I number also the painters, are obliged to create in the new sphere time-space constructions. As the new form of architecture has no place for fantasy (as expressed in separate painting or reliefs), the architect's intention from the very start is to create a harmonious whole with the essential means at his disposal, each architectural element contributing – on a practical and logical basis – to the creation of the greatest possible plastic expression without doing violence in

from its dependence on either large or small (as the use of the word 'monumental' has been exhausted, let us substitute the word 'plastic'). The new form has shown that everything depends on relationships, the relationship of one thing to another. 7. There is nothing passive about the new form of architecture. It has banished the problem of the hole in the wall. Windows have acquired an active significance by their openness as opposed to the closed-in character of the wall spaces. There is not a hole or an empty space anywhere, everything is strictly determined by its contrast value (compare the various contra-constructions in which the elements of architecture, plane, line, mass have been located, separately, in a three- any way to practical demands'.

Despite the similarity with Oud's ideas, a conflict arose because Van Doesburg with his ideas of 'spatial painting' wanted to combine architecture with the art of painting, whereas Oud felt that this would be to the detriment of architecture in the long run. Oud described in his book 'Mein Weg in "De Stijl"' how, when he built the holiday home 'De Vonk' in Noordwijkerhout in 1917, Van Does-burg designed a tiled floor for it and chose the colours in which the doors were to be painted. Oud said: 'That may well have been the first time that the doors of one room were painted in different colours with the idea of creating a spatial composition of forms. This was to result in a feeling of liberation in contrast to the feeling of restriction which is inherent in the nature of architecture.' He continued: 'We hoped that by painting the walls of small dwellings in different colours we could banish the cramped and oppressive atmosphere from a room and that it would consequently seem larger.

In deciding on the colours, consideration was also given to whether the light entered the room directly or obliquely. Nowadays, all that is taken as a matter of course. Then, it was quite revolutionary. In this field Van Doesburg really did pioneering work; and the more advanced colour schemes that were later developed in America, and which were based on psychological considerations, certainly owed something to the initiative of 'De Stijl'. However, a too intensive use of colour can do more harm than good.' Oud then points to Mondriaan's studio in New York as an example. To Oud's mind, the whole conception, as regards both the interior decorations and the furniture, is chaotic from the architect's point of view. He says: 'Mondriaan's 'spatial intent' is clearly evident, but his composition is that of a painter who lacks feeling for the aesthetic structure in architecture. While I was working with Van Doesburg, a conflict gradually arose between us, because his ideas were born of the unrestrained impulse of a painter, whereas I acknowledged the constraint that society lays upon style in practical building as one of the fundamental principles of the new form of architecture. Van Doesburg, for instance, designed white doors for some of my workmen's houses, although experience had taught me that my creations could have no lasting value if my design ignored the usual factors of everyday life. If a house is to be an asset to the community, it must be proof against dirty hands. A really fundamental difference between the painter's art and architecture comes to light when an architectural design whose effect depends on a number of doors being painted in the same colour is utterly marred by a colour scheme that totally disregards those architectural intentions. If, irrespective of the architectural aims, one door is painted blue and another yellow, an optical imbalance is created since the yellow door will seem to be much larger than the blue one. These are but a few of the many points on which we came to disagree, for the simple reason that the way in which form and colour had developed in 'De Stijl' was too free and, aesthetically speaking, too self-glorifying for it to remain in harmony with a healthy growth of architecture in our society. And without logical growth there could be no universal architecture, and no 'Stijl'!

The aesthetic attainments of 'De Stijl' were highly valuable. Fundamentally, they laid the foundations for a new form of architecture, but it had to prove under everyday conditions that it was socially justified.'

The architects of 'De Stijl' have, naturally enough, stayed more closely in touch with the requirements of society. Although their ideas were sober and business-like, few people had confidence in them and they did not receive many commissions. As a result, their ideas have a greater impact abroad than at home.

In that period Rietveld built his now very famous house in Utrecht (1924), which most certainly paved the way for the development of modern architecture; Oud built his houses in Tussendijken (1920), Oud-Mathenesse (1922), the Kiefhoek (1925), all in the Rotterdam area, and dwellings in the Hook of Holland (1924). Oud, Rietveld and Van Eesteren were the first to show the younger architects the road to a purer conception of architecture and it is certainly in part due to their influence that a new movement was born in 1927. The new group was cal-led 'The Eight' and consisted of eight Amsterdam architects, including Merkel-bach, Groenewegen, Boeken, Bijvoet, and Wiebenga. The third number of their magazine 'i 10' contained on page 126 a manifesto from the pen of B. Merkelbach, testifying to a more radical approach than the one already indicated by Oud. It contained the following statement:

What is 'The Eight'?

'The Eight' is the critical reaction to present-day architectural form.

'The Eight' is realistic in its endeavour to achieve immediate results.

'The Eight' is idealistic in its belief in international co-operation.

'The Eight' is opportunist by reason of social considerations.

'The Eight' is neither for nor against groups, persons or movements.

'The Eight' is only interested in facts.

'The Eight' affirms that, although it does not exclude the possibility of building in a beautiful style, it would be better to build for the time being in an ugly but

28

functional style than to put up show-piece façades that hide bad interior design. 'The Eight' wishes to subordinate itself to the requirements of its principals. 'The Eight' does not favour luxurious architecture that owes its origin to the delight which some talented individuals take in creating new forms.

'The Eight' wishes to be rational in the true sense, in other words, everything must be made subordinate to the requirements of the commission.

'The Eight' is attempting to find a social basis for modern architecture. (The architect à la mode is well on the way to becoming a luxury and an expensive tradition).

'The Eight' will restrict its campaign exclusively to professional circles.

'The Eight' is more concerned with developing the *science* than the *art* of architecture.

'The Eight' seeks to find a place in society as a creative organizer on a commercial footing.

'The Eight' is non-aesthetic.

'The Eight' is non-dramatic.

'The Eight' is non-romantic.

'The Eight' is non-cunbistic.

'The Eight' is a resultant force.

This Amsterdam group did not stand alone. Much earlier, in 1922, a group had been founded in Rotterdam under the name of 'Opbouw', which professed the same principles, and it is only natural that these two groups amalgamated, or at any rate resolved, after the first congress of the C.I.A.M. (Congrès Internationale d'Architecture Moderne) held in 1928 in La Saraz in Switzerland, to work in close co-operation with each other. Berlage, too, attended the Congress, which was clear proof of an affinity between him and the very latest group in Dutch architecture. In this way, international contacts were also officially re-established, and this movement, the new building style, the new rationalism, the functionalism, 'the international style' (a misleading term, actually), also called C.I.A.M.

architecture, has held its own to this day, although the C.I.A.M. as such was dissolved by the Congress held at Dubrovnik in 1956.

Meanwhile, another movement had started after the First World War, a movement that began by opposing the Amsterdam School, and later became the antithesis of the C.I.A.M. group. Its members were the architects who had lost their hearts to the old materials, timber and bricks, who wished to preserve handiwork, and who preached a return to old forms. They set great store by craftsmanship and spiritual tradition, and under their leader, M. J. Granpré Molière, who was appointed professor at Delft University in 1921 and who became a Roman Catholic in 1927, the movement became an important one, at least in the Netherlands, since it embraced aestheticism and ethical traditionalism as opposed to technical functionalism. The Delft School, as the movement was called, for the Delft Institute of Advanced Technology may properly be regarded as its cradle, can in some respects be attributed to Berlage's influence – when one remembers his love of artisanal purity – although it involves a tendency towards the romantic interpretation of history, to which Berlage was so much opposed. The Delft School condemned the C.I.A.M. group for being too materialistic; it comprised, however, a number of able architects, who were, to say the least, conservative. These architects enjoyed the confidence of their principals, so it is not surprising that many examples of their work are to be found throughout the country. Their work is not striking but it is of sound construction with a pronounced historical touch. The remarkable thing about the theories of the Delft School is that, according to Professor Granpré Molière, good architectural art should make use of rectangular as well as of curving and slanting planes and lines, ideas that came to the fore again in the years 1950–1960 in reaction to the all too rigid mathematical forms of functionalism, but were originally propounded for entirely different reasons.

The fact that the functionalists were forced back into a defensive position after 1930 was not only the work of the traditionalistic group, but also that of a younger group, which under the name of the '1932 Group' was originally, that is in 1934, affiliated with the Dutch C.I.A.M. group, in other words, with "De 8 en Opbouw'. But it loosened its ties with that group in 1938 in so far as a few older C.I.A.M. members left the movement, while some of the members of the '1932 Group' remained loyal to the C.I.A.M. The dissenters opposed the theory that a building represented the sum total of its requirements and were of opinion that the plastic art had to be reintroduced into architecture. Arthur Staal summarized his objections in the 'De 8 en Opbouw' magazine of 7th January, 1939, in the following sentence: 'We are afraid that the so-called 'orientation' may mean enslavement and regimentation of the mind'. Moreover, it could not be understood why a building should not be symmetrical or have a distinct façade, why decorations were taboo and why the monumental could not be countenanced. Many of the ideas held by this group were, however, founded on a certain misunderstanding of functionalism, which, although not rejecting beauty in form, did not make it the primary consideration. Among those who turned their backs on 'De 8 en Opbouw' were Staal, Komter, Groenewegen, Van Woerden, Holt, Elzas, Duintjer, Zanstra and Sijmons.

The members of the '1932 Group', who might be called functionalists, and who were converts to traditionalism, were, like the Delft traditionalists, conservative, and when they became active their work showed a fairly clear link with the Dutch classical Baroque style. Later they aimed at a more modern style, as evidenced by the designs submitted in the prize competition for a new Amsterdam Town Hall in 1937. These 'functional' traditionalists could therefore best be regarded as a group standing between the C.I.A.M. and the traditionalists.

The situation before World War II can be summarized as follows. The Amsterdam group was enjoying a late blossoming, thanks to the work of its epigones, but its influence was on the decline and, after World War II, no trace of it was left at all. Rietveld and Van Eesteren had deserted 'De Stijl' for the C.I.A.M.; Oud did not join and was much criticized by his former colleagues when, in 1938, he built the office for the Bataafse Import Maatschappij in The Hague. They cited Oud's own dictum of 1920: 'Ornamentation is the panacea for architectural impotence', and pointing to the building's entrance hall, they accused him of having there renounced his own principles. They reproached Oud that he cherished 'monumental' aspirations – a reproach that, as we have seen, weighed heavily with the Dutch. In recent years, however, Oud's 'deviation' has been receiving more appreciation, although admittedly the office building is a little too imposing for its surroundings and its purpose.

Encouraged by their success and strengthened by their convictions, the traditionalists proceeded on their chosen course, somewhat disjointedly and individualistically, and taking an occasional peep across the frontiers to see if anything to their liking was happening there. For instance, a few architects of this group were impressed with what was happening in Sweden and Germany, Enschede Town Hall (1933) and a few country houses being the result of that interest. There were also a few lone wolves such as Dudok, whose greatest success was his design for Hilversum Town Hall (1928). He was a typical individualist, who completely ignored all developments except his own. He did not form a 'school'; however, his latest works have much in common with the style of the moderate moderns.

The functional traditionalists, the '1932 Group', did not produce many important works before World War II, but the few examples there are clearly show the great influence Berlage had also on their work, especially as regards their use of beautiful brickwork walls. A few members of this group received awards for the designs they submitted for Amsterdam Town Hall in 1939, such as Duintjer and

Komter, and Arthur Staal, who produced a design jointly with his father, J. F. Staal. The C.I.A.M. produced a few excellent buildings, such as the 'Zonnestraal' Sanatorium (1928) by Bijvoet and Duiker; the Open Air School in Amsterdam (1931), the Third Technical Training School in Zwaardstraat, Scheveningen (1931) and Hotel 'Gooiland' (1936) by Duiker; the Van Nelle factory (1929–1930) by Brinkman and Van der Vlugt, which is now the classical example of modern Dutch architecture both at home and abroad; a school at Aalsmeer (1932) by J. G. Wiebenga; the houses in Vroesenlaan, Rotterdam (1934) by Van den Broek; the tall blocks of flats at Bergpolder (1933–1934) by Brinkman, Van Tijen and Van der Vlugt, and in Plaslaan (1938) by Van Tijen and Maaskant; blocks of houses in Erasmuslaan, Utrecht (1930–1931 and 1934), the Music School at Zeist (1932), a number of country houses and a cinema in Utrecht (1936) by Rietveld; the houses in Louise de Colignystraat in Amsterdam (1937) and the AVRO studio in Hilversum (1930) by Merkelbach and Karsten; the synagogue by Elzas in Lekstraat, Amsterdam (1936); and also buildings designed by A. Bodon, J. H. Groenewegen, J. B. van Loghem, and P. Elling. Some architects managed to achieve a remarkable cross between the style of the Amsterdam School and that of functionalism, a notable example being the 'De Volharding' building by J. W. E. Buys and J. B. Lürsen (1928). The fact that this list is not any longer shows that the modern architects, and especially Rietveld, did not receive the commissions and the recognition they deserved. However, even though the number of noteworthy buildings was fairly small, those there were secured for the Netherlands a good reputation abroad.

During the German occupation of the Netherlands, Dutch architects found themselves in a completely isolated position and, although there was much talk and even some sort of a conciliation between the C.I.A.M. architects, the traditionalists and the functional traditionalists, in the absence of building activity the situation remained static.

On the face of it, the various movements came closer together after World War II, for the latest technical devices and materials were then accepted also by the traditionalists. It is doubtful, though, whether this rapprochement truly occurred also in their conception of architectural art, and one cannot but wonder whether the traditionalists were prepared merely to utilize the new materials without comprehending their true essence and potential; in other words, they probably did not try to adapt their hardly changed outlook to the new aids, but attempted rather to force the new materials into the mould of their set ideas. It is our belief that the traditionalists accepted standardized building elements and industrialization of building methods out of sheer necessity; or rather, because of progress and changing times – not because of any inner compulsion. On the other hand, it would be wrong to prejudge the quality of a building according to whether the architect who designed it was slow or quick to adopt innovations, provided a well-considered use has been made of them and they were not employed as an afterthought.

An outsider can only follow and understand the often unfruitful and sometimes futile debate between the traditionalists, the moderns and those who cannot agree entirely with either side, if he realizes that architecture lies at the cross roads between art and science and that it has been in the throes of a crisis for decades.

The word 'crisis' should not be taken too dramatically; contrary to the situation in usual crises, the trouble here lies not so much in a shortage as in a surplus. We imagine that, with the great advances being made in science, we shall sooner or later be faced with the problem whether and, if so, how to utilize all the possibilities placed at our disposal, while the liberal arts, which have not changed in essence despite all the new methods of reproduction provided by radio, film and television, need only be concerned with the changes in the use of the various means of mass communication. Consequently, the problems with which the

34

liberal arts are faced will always remain fairly simple of solution despite the possible creation of all kinds of mixed forms for sound production, technical effects, pictures, speech, etc.

As its scope has widened, science has divided into various categories. The arts have remained what they were, and architecture, a combination of building technique and art, has been obliged to remain what it was, despite the fact that its field of activity has been expanding all the time while becoming less and less determinate. As a result of social and technological developments, architecture has to take so many more factors into account; it has been given so many more functions, so to speak, that the work of an architect has become extremely complex. The acceptance of new technical aids in architecture involves far greater tensions than arise when a new kind of equipment is to be built or new production methods are to be introduced. For the new equipment will hardly ever be the final product; there is a general belief that sooner or later it will be improved upon and, before very long, will probably be superseded. A building, on the other hand, whether a factory or a town hall, a block of flats or a church, is regarded as the final product, just the same as a work of art.

It is only in recent years that people have been coming to the conclusion that buildings whose function or construction no longer served the purpose for which they were built – in other words, buildings which had become more or less obsolete – needed to be replaced. But, because of their architectural beauty we are prevented from demolishing them to clear the site for a new building; so it is decided to repair them and to find a 'suitable', which very often proves to be an 'unsuitable', use for them. For instance, they are frequently converted into museums, whereby the character of the building is impaired.

Yet it is often not only the architectural beauty, but also the money invested in an old building that prevents us from taking rapid action and putting a new one in its place. An architect is therefore bound to take account of possible trends quite far into the future.

That is why architects, more than any other artists or scientists, must be prepared to engage in speculation. The buildings they create must remain useful – and beautiful – for seventy-five or a hundred years, and in some cases even longer. Whereas the scientist and the technician, who as far as their creative work is concerned may be bracketed together, can rely on a tradition, on an unbroken chain made up of those who go before and those who come after, and can content themselves with a provisional conclusion, the artist must, somehow, reach a final conclusion: the work of art. The architect is, therefore, obliged to perform a two-sided task – he must utilize the technical means at his disposal at a given moment (with which he can, after all, only reach a provisional conclusion), but must, at the same time, reach a final conclusion, (represented by the building project, the work of art).

It is therefore not surprising that, in view of technical advances, the architect is not always able to mould his means into the forms they should be given. In other words, many architects are not sufficiently conversant with the problems of construction to be able to find the proper form for it. Professor B. H. H. Zweers formulated the problem as follows in a speech entitled 'Concrete people and human concrete', which was reproduced in the 'De Ingenieur' magazine of 16th January, 1953: 'The combination of artist and precise thinker is rarely to be found in any one human being. So it is that architecture is based on beauty of form and the superficial properties of the building materials. Buildings are no longer *constructed*, they are *calculated*. For misfortunes never come singly; modern techniques make it possible to do *anything* with new materials. The building, no matter how ridiculous its construction may be, is erected on the basis of such thorough calculations that it is guaranteed not to collapse. This has decided the fate of constructional methods, which, on the one hand, have become too complicated for the architect, and, on the other, are so clever that they put practically no limitations on architectural possibilities'. Many architects are in wholehearted agreement with these sentiments.

In this day and age, we can hardly deny the truth of Professor Zweers' ideas; it would be otherwise if modern techniques developed less rapidly and permitted us to keep up with them so that we could give freer rein to our *imagination* when building. However, we ought to remember that even though the form may be largely determined by the construction, it should be possible to invest a sound construction with a variety of forms.

It should also be remembered that if we were to arrange matters in hierarchical order, it would at any rate be the function that determined the *choice* of construction. If, as an able architect told me, an architect could choose freely between a steel frame and a concrete frame, he would give preference to the latter because it would leave him more freedom in the choice of design. If, however, a factory has to be built with an eye to the possibility of later modification and extension, a steel frame is to be preferred. But, if the factory has to house a chemical works, where the fumes might affect the steel structures, the choice would not be quite so easy, and somebody who knows little or nothing of construction matters will have to make a decision based on completely different considerations from those that would suggest themselves to a building engineer.

Though it may be true that the construction is one of the factors that determine the design, it is at any rate an *ancillary factor*, for, should construction and function come into conflict, then construction *must* always take second place. Take, for example, our modern railway stations. The fact that they look so different from those built at the end of the nineteenth century is purely a matter of function, determined by the changes resulting from the almost complete electrification of the railways.

The relative values of the three 'elements' of the old trinity, function, construction and design, originally considered equal, were changed by Sullivan (or rather by Greenough) by the dictum 'Form follows function'. Professor Zweers added to that 'Form follows construction'. That is all well and good, but in this way elements, which imperceptibly combine to create a harmonious unit, are being forcibly separated. A discussion on the subject would be just as futile as a discussion on a literary work where the object was to decide whether the form or the content should be the predominating factor. I do not want to dismiss the subject by saying that neither should predominate, quoting the well-known dictum that there should be harmony. In architecture things are different because the elements are separate in one way or another, each demanding a different kind of knowledge, and imagination. And architecture is such a difficult profession for the very reason that all these factors must culminate in one work of art, a work of art that can be viewed from different angles.

It will often depend on the commission whether and to what degree the design, the function or the construction is the predominating factor. In the case of a small chapel the function is so 'small' and the construction so simple that design can be said to be paramount; in the case of a church where the representative part of the external appearance and the creation of an atmosphere of sanctity are the dominant factors, the design will determine the function in part, but it will wholly determine the construction. A town hall is different again; there the representative part of the external appearance and inner atmosphere can be said to predominate to a lesser extent over the function, while the administrative part is wholly determined by the function.

Function determines the design of a factory or office, but, in the case of a bridge, construction is the most important factor. It could be argued that in these examples the three elements have not been kept entirely separate. I do not mind admitting that this is true; in fact, it was what I intended to demonstrate.

Just how complicated these notions are and how easily they may cause confusion within the profession itself is illustrated by J. M. Richards in his book entitled 'An Introduction to Modern Architecture'. He writes: 'There is an idea called 'functionalism' that is often associated with modern architecture; in fact even by well-informed people modern architecture is often described as 'functionalist'. As this description is entirely untrue it may be as well, before we continue our examination of the actual effect of machine production on architectural design, to give some attention to laying this particular bogey.

It is difficult to say when the idea of functionalism was first put about. It is present, with reservations, in many writings about architecture from the Roman Vitruvius onwards; but in these cases, of course, the reservations are all-important. For architecture, being a practical art, must always depend to some degree on function, a fact which all sensible writers on the subject have recognized. But the idea of absolute functionalism – which can be defined as the idea that good architecture is produced automatically by strict attention to utility, economy and other purely practical considerations – is a more recent phenomenon. It is doubtful, as a matter of fact, whether this theory in its absolute form has ever been seriously held by practising architects; they would soon have found that it prevented them from exercising their functions at all.'

Richards further states that the technique is purely functional and that architecture is more than that. All this is undoubtedly true, but in my opinion it would nevertheless be possible to term present-day architecture functionalist in so far as it answers present-day needs. For when the nineteenth-century architects were faced with new tasks, such as the designing of stations, department stores, museums and post offices, they could find no other solution than to build them in the old familiar styles, in other words, they failed to find adequate forms for the functions of those buildings. The modern architect who understands his calling, his profession, will give pride of place to the subject of his commission, that is, to the function of the building he is to design; the design and construction will be secondary considerations. It will, however, be readily agreed that an architect may visualize everything at the same time, in a sudden flash, and that the designing of a building is not the same as working out a mathematical problem whose solution is 'beautiful'.

But Richards goes on to say: 'Even after we have said that it is engineering which is functional and architecture which is something more, it is often difficult to decide where the one begins and the other ends. The 'something more' means that architectural design includes decisions or preferences made for non-utilitarian reasons, but we find that in all but the very simplest engineering problems room is also left for taste or preference to enter: choosing between certain alternatives or consciously varying the result within certain limits. Even engineering itself, that is to say, is seldom truly functional. The explanation of this difficulty is of course that the distinction between engineering and architecture is entirely an artificial one. It is only a hundred years old, having come about when the academic architects became primarily engrossed in styles early in the nineteenth century; when they came to regard the language of architecture as an end in itself instead of as a means to an end.'

This prominent English critic of architecture thus sides, albeit with a certain hesitation, with those who consider that architectural design is determined just as much by the 'function' of the building in question as is the building technique by the function of the structure.

It becomes no more than a word-play if one goes beyond the simple statement that the design is determined by the function and/or the construction, while the commission, which for an architectural design may be of almost unlimited variety, determines to some extent the relationship between 'technique' and 'science' on the one hand and 'technique' and 'art' on the other. At the same time, it is of course understood that designing a work of architectural art requires a large measure of creativity.

Besides engineering techniques, social consciousness has unmistakably penetrated the field of architecture. We may take it for granted that the planner must be first and foremost a sociologist, even though it might be argued that planning most certainly involves a 'shaping of the location of human settlements', but the town planner enters the field of architecture before he is aware of it, as evidenced by the squabble between town planners and architects as to the part that each is to play. Although it is no doubt true that planning the layout of a town, which certainly is to some degree 'architectural' work, will largely determine the shape of a district, it could hardly be argued that the architecture of the buildings themselves does not play an important role. Where architecture ends and town planning begins has by no means been decided as yet; it is, for instance, impossible to say whether the laying out of a public garden, the design of a basement, the building of pathways and playgrounds and the effect they will have on the surroundings should be left to the architect or to the town planner to decide. The whole question of housing, including standardization, industrialized and system building, has become an architectural cum town-planning problem, and nobody will dispute the fact that the social requirements of an office or factory form part of the function of such a building and that they therefore automatically play a part in determining its design. To take into account the social requirements, to have a thorough knowledge of technical aids, to design a 'functional' building and yet create a work of architectural art that appeals to the eye and will not become decrepit after a certain time constitutes a task of such magnitude that it cannot possibly be performed by one man, the only solution being to form a group, or a team as it is called.

However, the disadvantages of working as a group are obvious. Every expert will quite honestly and with the best intentions in the world consider his own field the most important, or, at any rate, he will have a better insight into the problems in his own particular field. Democracy is not feasible in such a situation: in the end, one man will have to take the responsibility and, traditionally, that man is the architect.

The architect, in continual consultation with the town planner and the sociologist, the heating-system expert and the constructor, the maker of the standard elements for system building, the maker of standardized components, the building engineer and the house-painter, has to make a blue-print that is the synthesis of his and their ideas. He must anticipate the future while giving the present its due; his work should not be so futuristic that his contemporaries, unable to appreciate it, fail to make good use of it. He must not be afraid of copying details or even the main features of his predecessors, for architecture is a traditional art; but whatever he adopts from them he should embody in his own plan in his own way, or else be accused of plagiarism. He must be able to visualize the possible extension of a building or even of a complex of buildings; he should even be able, as J. P. Mieras remarked in "Bouwkundig Weekblad" of 20th to 27th December, 1955, in respect of the Tomado factory at Etten-Leur, to design a building that is not only unfinished but also shows in its ground-plan that it is not intended ever to become a rounded-off architectural entity in the traditional sense.

It is the need to be a realist and yet a visionary which makes the present-day architect such a fascinating personality – though sometimes vague and aggressive in his statements. For the realm of the future cannot be entered with impunity by scientist or artist; he turns his back on reality and begins to speculate, and speculators are invariably wrong because they are ignorant and indeed wish to be ignorant of a great number of factors. The number of possible solutions becomes so great that every guiding principle gets bogged down in a morass of possibilities and nobody will agree with anybody else however closely related their points of departure may be.

That is one of the reasons why the formerly united caste of architects has disintegrated into groups, or rather into individuals, divided by differences in technical knowledge, in social ideas, in their philosophy of life.

This accounts for such slogans as 'we must not allow the technical side of building to get the upper hand', while that technical side is part of ourselves, or 'we must control nature', while the creative element must rely entirely on what nature provides, or 'we are entering a new cultural phase', while we know that every cultural phase is a transitional phase in which man himself hardly changes. Most of those slogans can be attributed to an exaggeration of the importance of events in any sphere during the period in which we happen to live.

One of the results of the conflicting opinions as to the relative importance of function and construction, or construction and design, is that it has become essential to specialize. The profession of architect was first divided up into town planners and architects, but the latter group seems to have split up still further into housing specialists (sub-divided into designers of traditional dwellings and designers of system-built dwellings), railway-station specialists, factory designers, bridge designers, market-hall designers, hospital designers, department-store designers, etc., one category placing the emphasis on the function and the other on the construction. There is perhaps still a 'free' sector for the designing of country houses, churches, office buildings, shops, town halls, etc., where it is easy to concentrate on the function and/or the construction.

Generally, however, it seems that a choice must inevitably be made between intensive specialization and working as a team.

In all this it should also be borne in mind that a building is tied to a certain location; the climate, the nature of the ground and the population play a role in determining the design, and these factors may well accentuate any differences that already exist. It is also a fact that architects who are not wholly enthusiastic about the new technical aids but accept them out of necessity, and who are at the same time more inclined to be conservative than progressive in their social outlook, are apt to place the emphasis on the 'local colour' of a particular region or country. One is justified in wondering whether the one follows logically from the other; whether it follows automatically that the advocates of tradition in architecture who are conservative in their social outlook are nationally minded, whereas the champions of new methods and ideas in architecture and in the social sphere are internationally minded. On the face of things it would seem to be so, but on closer consideration of the matter one begins to have one's doubts.

For the question arises whether there has ever been a purely national or a purely international style, whether the style was adapted to a particular region and its population or whether it was simply continued and further developed. Examples taken from classical antiquity, Gothic and Renaissance art, in short, from all the various periods, are proof that there is some truth in both and that it is not exclusively a question of adaptation or of continuation. The Meat-market hall in Haarlem and the Pazzi Chapel in Florence are poles apart, yet both of them belong to the Renaissance period; whereas there is a strong similarity between the court-yards of the Military Academy at Breda and the Ducal Palace at Urbino, or the Palazzo Valmarana at Vicenza and the Mauritshuis in The Hague.

Eclecticism, imitation of style, has always been an international phenomenon, and although we do not object to its manifestation in the Renaissance period, it is frowned upon when it intrudes upon the nineteenth-century style. And there are very good reasons for that, too, for the 'imitation' Renaissance buildings are most acceptable, whereas the nineteenth-century copies are not; but this has nothing to do with the question whether the architects were internationally minded or not, because both groups were! The Renaissance itself was 'eclectic', having borrowed freely from classical architecture. In other words, it is immaterial where the architect gets his 'examples' from (and no artist can do without examples and predecessors); the result depends on his personality.

In theory, then, there are unlimited opportunities for developing one's own style, but many moderns are often too much inclined to follow the old ways blindly and to neglect their duty, which should consist in developing new designs with the new aids at their disposal, and in paying due heed to the requirements of the surroundings. The traditionalists, on the other hand, are too much inclined to impose the narrow limits of their own imagination upon the new aids, and to overestimate the requirements of the surroundings. One group will thus drift towards international eclecticism and the other towards provincial eclecticism. There are examples of both these groups in post-war Dutch architecture.

It should here be emphasized that the difference between the traditionalists and the moderns is not merely a divergence of opinion on architectural art, but also a difference in the way the two groups view life in general. The traditionalists, with their preference for the 'closed-in space' show thereby that they also favour a 'closed community', the family, and the religious community. The moderns, on the other hand, believe that, partly as a result of the developments in the field of transportation, the world has become a smaller place and therefore can and should constitute one large community. This conviction is reflected in the idea of the 'open space', the 'continuous space', which fosters closer contact between people. The conflict is a sharp one, each party maintaining its own point of view in an almost orthodox fashion.

Results obtained during the first few years after World War II were not encouraging. In the reconstruction plans for Middelburg and Rhenen, two towns that were badly damaged early in the war, the planners seemed to lack the courage to design new centres, and they rebuilt in a style that was also architecturally 'archaic', disregarding or misinterpreting present-day requirements to such an extent that even the traditionalists were shocked. This, too, was a clear illustration of the strong connection between architecture and town planning.

A town plan, whether it is a reconstruction plan, a town-centre renewal plan or an extension plan, will, despite all the expert research work preceding its execution, breathe the spirit of the architect and be determined by the quality of his work. The first reconstruction plans of the many damaged Dutch towns were wholly traditionalistic; there was a wish to revive the past, with the result that also in other towns, besides the two just mentioned, streets were built which, from an architectural point of view, are now considered totally inadequate. It was fortunate, in a way, that the reconstruction programme, and generally speaking all building activities, made a slow start in the first few years owing to shortage of money and materials. In the period 1945-1950, only a few buildings of any importance were built; most of the buildings erected were warehouses, factories and shops. It was not until after 1950 that Dutch architecture began to flourish again, and this revival was largely due to the challenge presented to architects by Rotterdam's ambitious reconstruction programme. It may seem a little strange to postulate that a highly intellectual activity, such as architectural creation undoubtedly is, depends on economic conditions, but the simple fact is that architecture is largely dependent on the opportunities to concretize certain concepts, and the exchange of ideas between the architect and his client – where the town planner, too, can very often make his influence felt – is a primary condition for a satisfactory result. In Rotterdam there was a team of town planners and also a number of businessmen who were not afraid of an enlargement in the scale of their town.

They specified their requirements accordingly, and collaborated in fulfilling them; a link-up was consequently made with a trend that had been followed in the Netherlands – but only very hesitatingly – ever since 1930. The answer given by the traditionalist architects to that challenge was most unsatisfactory, and only when it was realized how miserably they were failing in their attempts to force new techniques into the old forms or to compromise in the use of those techniques, was it suddenly remembered that other architects were to be found in the Netherlands who produced designs much bolder than those of their conservative colleagues. Had they also failed, Dutch architecture would have reverted to the provincialism into which it had sunk before 1940. To give a few traditionalists their due, it should be stated that they, too, were fully aware of the requirements of a new town in modern times, and they made praiseworthy efforts to make up for lost time. This explains why the building style of Rotterdam gradually became more and more up to date without showing obvious signs of foreign borrowings. One can see the reflection, as it were, of the development of architecture in the Netherlands in that important city. The first few buildings, a few banks and warehouses in the centre of the town, were built in the same style as the buildings which they replaced, while also the first shops surmounted by dwellings show no trace of architectural imagination. As one proceeds in time, however, the architecture shows considerable improvement. Remarkable examples are the multi-purpose buildings of an entirely new type, designed by Van Tijen and Maaskant, in which small industries and wholesale offices and showrooms were housed. At first these buildings were in the style of old Dutch warehouses, but the most recent ones took on a new form entirely their own. The same development can be observed in the shops. Van den Broek and Bakema started with a building that housed three separate shops, which was faintly reminiscent of the Amsterdam School; their last work was the Lijnbaan shopping centre reserved for pedestrians, intersected by tall blocks of flats, which has become famous all over the world. In Rotterdam one encounters a new use of old ideas, such as small one-storey shops standing like booths on the pavements. Much thought was given to town-planning problems, such as the question of a general enlargement of scale, the solution of which had its repercussions on the architecture. Rotterdam's example soon fired enthusiasm elsewhere. Nimeguen, Groningen, Hengelo, and also parts of Arnhem, Enschede and Zutphen were rebuilt in a much better fashion than one had dared to hope, although the standard set by Rotterdam was seldom reached and then only in a few isolated buildings.

Besides the problems attaching to the reconstruction of the country, the Dutch were faced with the task of building farms and villages in its new polders, which, as the former Zuyder Zee, now Lake Yssel, was gradually reclaimed, had to be settled. The farms, built up from pre-fabricated components, have a traditional form and it does not seem likely that modern designs will oust this old well-tried building style in the future, although some young architects are making an interesting study of the subject. The villages, too, are from an architectural point of view traditional rather than modern, with the exception of Nagele in the North-East Polder, which was planned by a C.I.A.M. group, the architectural designs of the buildings themselves also being made by C.I.A.M. architects.

The rebuilding of partly destroyed towns and the erection of new buildings in reclaimed areas is fascinating work, and much more remains to be done in this field, now that the centre of Rotterdam has been practically completed, in the areas south-west of that city, where, as part of the Delta Project, new towns will be built, while many villages will still have to be built in the Lake Yssel polders. But equally important are the extension plans of the towns, which owing to the rapid increase in the country's population and the continuing process of industrialization often increase the number of their inhabitants by 30 per cent or more. A few places that once were sleepy little towns, such as Emmen, Delfzijl and Vlaardingen have rapidly become towns of some importance, either on account of their industrialization, or because they are situated, like Vlaardingen, on the water-way connecting Rotterdam with the sea; and many of them, especially Vlaardingen and Emmen, now boast buildings that are of considerable architectural interest.

The new districts, of course, consist largely of blocks of dwellings and the lay-outs of the flats have undergone great changes. Although here, too, town planning considerations have greatly influenced the architecture, it must be admitted that on the whole the external design of the buildings has not been very successful. Whether this is due to the high building costs or to lack of interest on the part of the architects, the fact remains that the blocks of flats are as a general rule monotonous. However, much has been done to improve the interior arrangement of the dwellings. They usually comprise a living-room, a kitchen, a shower, a bedroom for the parents and one or more bedrooms for the children, and each flat has its own cellar on the ground or basement floor, which has superseded the customary attic. Compared with various other countries, especially the Scandinavian ones, Dutch dwellings are generally rather poorly equipped; more often than not there is no central rubbish disposal arrangement, nor are they centrally heated or provided with other modern facilities. New houses and flats in the Netherlands are small in comparison with many new dwellings in France (e.g. Sarcelles and Beauregard near Paris) and England (Roehampton, near London). However, new housing schemes that from an architectural point of view are fairly satisfactory are to be found sporadically among the many mediocre buildings in various towns, like Groningen, Amersfoort (several blocks by Zuiderhoek), Vlaardingen ('Babberspolder' and 'Westwijk' by Van Tijen and Groosman), Schiedam (by Groosman), Amsterdam ('Frankendaal' by Merkelbach and Elling; also dwellings by Aldo van Eyck, Groenewegen,

Kloos, Bodon and Zanstra in 'Slotermeer'; in 'Osdorp', 'Slotervaart' and 'Geuzenveld' dwellings by Van den Broek and Bakema – very much neglected since they were built a few years ago – by Salomonson, Van Gool, Staal, Dudok, Van Tijen, Bodon, Berghoef, Stam and Bijvoet); but unfortunately there are also many ugly buildings to be seen in those new outlying districts of Amsterdam. Further good examples are to be found in Leyden (by Groosman), Rotterdam (in 'Zuidwijk', 'Pendrecht' and in the centre by Van den Broek and Bakema, Bakker, Krijgsman, Boks, Maaskant, and Van Tijen), Utrecht (in the vicinity of Herderplein by Groosman; in 'Hoograven' by Rietveld; on 'Kanaleneiland' by Fledderus and others).

In the fourth number of 1960–1961 of the 'Forum' Magazine, J. B. Bakema made some generally valid observations regarding the building of houses and flats. He wrote: 'If makers of pre-fabricated building components were to co-operate with each other, it would be possible to manufacture interchangeable parts, which would mean more variety in interior design than is at present possible. In the absence of such co-operation, modern building techniques offer much less choice where the design of dwellings is concerned than was the case in former days when builders were limited in their material to bricks.

A population group that before 1920 received scant heed now occupies most of the new urban extensions built with government subsidy after the war. It is this very section of the population that is told that choosing one's personal style of living is one of the characteristics of Western democracy and that this privilege is worth fighting for. But the dwellings built for them offer, in actual fact, much less choice in this respect than ever before.

The density of the population in the Netherlands makes it imperative that the housing of people in tall blocks of flats be embodied in a well-co-ordinated plan with other forms of housing at ground level and at the necessary intermediate levels, so as to maintain, as much as possible, the aspect of a spacious landscape in people's daily lives. This can be achieved only if town-planning and architectural aspects are properly co-ordinated.' And further on: 'It should first of all be realized in much wider circles than purely among architects how much damage is being done at present in the Netherlands owing to the fact that our houses have become nothing more than places for beds, plus a few extra cubic meters for us to move about in, the earlier conception of a house as a place where people could meet in spacious surroundings having gone entirely by the board.

Bakema mentions the possibilities offered by system building, which has not yet made much headway in the Netherlands. This may be due to lack of experience, the large number of systems, and the fact that no system has yet been invented that reduces building costs to any great extent.

For some time now, only a very mild interest has been shown in pre-fabricated building, but it has recently begun again to claim a fair amount of attention. Van den Broek and Bakema, Van Tijen, Groosman, Klein, Berghoef and Zwiers are among the architects who have availed themselves most of this building technique, some of them using Dutch, others using foreign systems.

In his article entitled 'Architecture of this Century' (in the series 'The Beauty of our Country' published by Contact of Amsterdam in 1959), Mr. J. J. Vriend wrote about the possibilities and the future of system building: 'The need to introduce system building has now become particularly urgent because of the shortage of skilled workers in the building trade. It is generally of little or no interest to the building world as a modern method. (It is significant, though, that a few years ago an Association of System Builders was formed in the Netherlands and was joined by eighteen of the most important companies in that field, something that in the immediate post-war years would have been unthinkable.) The building trade is made up of a community that has grown over the years into a practically independent body with its own unwritten laws and mutual or conflicting interests. Building has thus become a process in which psychological and purely business considerations play their part in turn or simultaneously. The part played therein by 'the authorities' should not be underestimated. Where an official body has the final say in the choice between the traditional method and system building, and that body is by inclination or by upbringing traditionally minded, purely personal preference may decide the issue if the costs involved are the same in either case. If, however, system building is seen to be cheaper, the person in authority will have to wrestle with his conscience, for it is also his duty to be as economical as possible with public funds. That is understandable and only human.

It has been generally agreed for decades that a kitchen built from pre-fabricated components has great advantages over a kitchen built by traditional methods, but it has taken quite some time for this belief to be put into practice.

It is inevitable that system building will gain currency in the long run and the dividing line between the fields in which system building and the traditional method are to be adopted will become clearer in the course of time. This is all the more understandable when we realize that both commerce and engineering are, throughout the world, encroaching further and further upon what was once the exclusive domain of the architect. It is nowadays even frequently said in commercial and technical circles that, at any rate where house-building is concerned, architects have become superfluous! This is a very dangerous situation. No matter how far the techniques of building are perfected, it is the architect who has the last word in the lay-out and design. If, for instance, for 'practical' reasons, the building of houses were left to the commercial-technical sector, our new towns would be no more than a collection of barracks and arbitrary box-like structures.

The large house-building companies throughout the world ceased long ago to be the genial contractors they were, and now dominate the building economy. But they, too, must be made to realize that their work also affects what we call people's sense of beauty. That is undoubtedly an advantage of our times.'

A great danger of system building is that technical progress is not yet such that it can do full justice to what we term ideal housing conditions. When, for example, large pre-fabricated components are used which have to be put into place by a gantry crane, it is necessary, for reasons of efficiency and economy, to construct large blocks of dwellings, and this makes for monotony in the urban scene. Moreover, system building allows hardly any variation in the façade; worse still, it restricts the possibilities of varying the ground-plan.

Although it should be possible to perfect system building, a lot still has to be done before houses can be built that meet the very widely divergent wishes of the public. Not only will the number and size of the rooms and a functional lay-out of the dwelling have to be given careful attention, but the possibility must also be examined of providing each member of the family, the parents as well as the children, with adequate 'play' space.

Special attention has been given in the Netherlands to homes for the aged. In this country, with its low death rate (and its very high birth rate), they have sprung up like mushrooms, but neither their architecture nor their ground-plans have always been satisfactory. Homes for the aged are something entirely new, and, what is more, they are destined for an exceptionally sensitive group of the population. Without minimizing the work of others, it may be said that W. van Tijen, who has also done yeoman's service in establishing proper standards for working-class housing, has, in collaboration with other architects, designed some excellent homes such as have seldom been equalled. These homes should, of course, present a quiet, modest and peaceful aspect and architects have in general managed to avoid reproducing the atmosphere of the almshouse court-yards of the past, which are still a feature of many old town centres in the Netherlands, and where the aged remain more or less shut in and isolated from everyday life.

As regards many other public buildings, we should once again point out that the Dutch are a people very much divided into denominational groups. So it is that in the Netherlands there are State schools, to which parents who do not belong to any religious sect generally send their children, and Protestant schools for children from Protestant families. Since the Protestants are themselves divided into various sects, one finds in many municipalities separate primary, secondary, and also technical schools for these different sects in addition to the State schools. Lastly, there are the Roman Catholic primary and secondary schools. Grammar schools, both classical and modern, show the same variety, while there is even a Roman Catholic University in Nimeguen and a Protestant one in Amsterdam – besides the 'neutral' Municipal and State Universities.

It is easy to imagine what the results of this far-going fragmentation are. The various communities are fairly small, although in some places and regions a certain religion predominates (such as Roman Catholicism in the South), so that the schools, churches and other community centres are also generally small. This means that 'comprehensive schools' such as exist in England are very rare in the Netherlands. It does sometimes happen that an infant school, a primary school and a secondary school are built on the same plot of land, but their administration and organization is kept strictly separate, so that they form a unit only as far as the architectural and town-planning aspects are concerned. The result: small schools and many schools. There is hardly an architect in the Netherlands who has not at some time or other built a school. One can hardly speak of a special style, nor of systematic joint research resulting in a preference for a particular type of school building. There is no fixed 'line' in school building, the advantage of this being that surprisingly successful 'individual styles' are able to evolve. Because the Dutch are greatly interested in the education of their children, there are many well-appointed and well-designed schools with roomy, airy classrooms. There are good schools to be found throughout the country, designed, for example, by Van Eyck (Nagele), by Maaskant (Meppel and The Hague), by Wilhelm (Groningen), by Romke de Vries (Sneek), by Schamhart (The Hague), by Vegter (Delfzijl and Groningen), by Schenk (Utrecht), by Zuiderhoek (Amersfoort), by Van den Broek and Bakema (Rotterdam), and by Oud (The Hague) and many others, far too numerous to mention.

It is, of course, even more complicated when it comes to churches; there are many small churches of different religious sects. Only in a few places in the North are the Protestants so homogeneous that large churches can be built; in the South, on the other hand, the Roman Catholics are usually well able to build sizeable churches. Modern town-planning, which tends to provide for new districts that are strictly separate the one from the other, does not make for the building of large churches, even where the population happens to be homogeneous.

It is possibly because of this lack of opportunity that church building in the Netherlands has not yet found its style. However, the Protestants have felt the need, much earlier than the Roman Catholics, to give their churches an entirely new form. The Calvinist Protestant Church, faced with the necessity of building a great many churches, found the time opportune to give serious consideration to new forms, inspiration being often quite unintentionally sought in the architecture of Dutch Protestant churches of the seventeenth and eighteenth centuries, a style which had been much underrated both at home and abroad. These churches were generally small because the pulpit was the focal point and the minister's voice had to be audible to the whole congregation; although they were products of classicism, they had a character of their own. They are of a highly unorthodox style with ground-plans in the form of squares, circles and Greek crosses, or of even more complicated mathematical design, as was quite usual in the classical Baroque style. The general impression, however, is severe and confined, in keeping with the spirit of early Protestantism. The modern counterpart is more friendly, more peaceful and gentler, yet retains a certain confinedness and dignity. Unlike other countries, however, the Netherlands has not dared to indulge in real experiments. Despite the use of concrete, and even cellular concrete, design has remained carefully conservative and one will look in vain in the Netherlands for anything similar to the chapel in Ronchamp, or work that is even remotely akin to that of Frank Lloyd Wright, Niemeyer, Andrault or Candela, who could obviously give much freer rein to their fancies. The Protestants were carefully feeling their way towards new forms, mostly under the guidance of their ministers, who often had great difficulty in persuading their more conservative parishioners.

The best proof of their diligent search for a satisfactory solution is the fact that several architects were invited to design a chapel for the 'Kerk en Wereld' Society (The Church and World). An exhibition was made of the designs they submitted and an award was given for the best entry. The architects approached were P. Blom – who later withdrew from the competition – G. Boon, A. E. van Eyck, H. Hertzberger, E. J. Jelles, J. van Stigt and J. Verhoeven. It was the work of Aldo van Eyck that was finally selected for execution. Although the designs submitted were generally interesting, it can hardly be said that they would have been regarded as having a pioneering quality in other countries, such as

Brazil, France, Germany or Spain. Without wishing to question in any way the talent of the participants, we are bound to state that in the Netherlands a large number of would-be modern churches have been designed in accordance with a more or less fixed present-day code, and that the younger architects in particular have been given little opportunity to try their hand at church design.

Where the Roman Catholics are concerned it should be stated that only in the beginning of the nineteenth century were they allowed to build churches again in the Netherlands. And their new churches were of necessity imitative in style. Since it was not possible to build on a strong tradition – during the Baroque period Catholicism was in a somewhat underprivileged position – and even before the Reformation church-builders in the Netherlands were wholly dependent for their inspiration on the surrounding countries, the opportunity – or courage – to break with tradition was lacking and the tendency was to adhere to old forms. It is true that before World War II Boosten made a few successful attempts to rejuvenate Roman Catholic church building in the Netherlands, but after 1945 the traditional forms were reverted to, save for the occasional creation by Peutz or Holt. The reaction to lack of tradition was an excessive love of tradition and the results were not very happy: stark piles of brick, imitation Romanesque, making in general a very dull impression. The Roman Catholics themselves were not very satisfied with these churches and in 1958 they began to give frank and serious consideration to evolving a new style of church building. Public and private discussions soon bore fruit and Roman Catholic church building is now undergoing rapid changes. Striking churches have been built, for example in Zevenaar (by Starmans), Valkenburg (by Boosten), Volendam (by Oudejans and Alberts), and in The Hague (by Taen and Nix).

Since in churches there should be a close relationship between the building and its atmosphere, with the architect, unencumbered by considerations of utility, otherwise left free to choose his design, one might have expected that developments in the Netherlands, where a large part of the population is sincerely religious, would have been much more characteristic of the country, as they were, for example, in Switzerland. Although this was not in fact the case, the average achievement was on a higher level than one might conclude from the lack of outstanding examples. It is possible that the realization that nothing much has yet been achieved in this field may prove an incentive to produce more impressive work in the future. There are already some hopeful signs that such a development is now under way.

There has been remarkable development in industrial building in the Netherlands, which is all the more striking when one considers that the country industrialized late, its income being derived principally from trade and agriculture. However, the loss of markets and the loss of their colonies compelled the Dutch to seek other sources of income, and after World War II industrial expansion was actively promoted by the Government, despite the fact that almost all raw materials have to be imported. The architecture of industrial buildings such as factories, offices, shops, laboratories, railway stations and dock warehouses is generally of a fairly high standard; in this field, too, the average is good and there are no outstanding buildings (such as the Van Nelle factory built in the 'thirties). It is also noteworthy that other industrial building not usually directly associated with architecture, such as the construction of bridges, dams, locks and lockhouses, street furniture, etc., is being taken in hand with particular care. Foreign expert opinion on Dutch post-war architecture, is, on the whole, not unfavourable, but it is thought that the standard achieved in the glorious years between 1920 and 1930 when the Netherlands was leading the field, has not been equalled. U. Kultermann, for instance, in 'Bouwkunst van deze tijd' (Present-day Architecture), published by N.V. Uitgeversmaatschappij Kosmos, Amsterdam-Antwerp, 1958, wrote: 'The best-known example of Dutch post-war architecture is a shopping centre, the 'Lijnbaan', in Rotterdam. The approach of the architects J. H. van den Broek and J. B. Bakema was entirely new. They built several 'streets' of shops from which they banned all traffic. All the shops are single-storeyed and have been built to the same design. From the point of view of town planning too, Rotterdam is an excellent example of how the centre of a big town should be rebuilt. The architects H. Maaskant, H. Krijgsman and H. D. Bakker have contributed greatly to this success with their high blocks of flats. E. F. Groosman has built excellent flats in Schiedam.

The great tradition of Dutch architecture in the 'twenties and 'thirties was not maintained at the same level in later years. It is true that the standard of Dutch architecture is still fairly high today, but there is no denying that the élan of the 'twenties has been superseded by a more conservative attitude; there is even a certain stagnation. The pioneers no longer point the way. It is true that J. J. P. Oud has designed interesting schools and that Rietveld's Museum of Sculpture in Arnhem (since 1965 rebuilt at Otterlo) introduced new ideas in the field of museum architecture, but these achievements have failed to inspire a later generation. The young Dutch architects, like Haan and Van Eyck, are still searching for points of contact with international trends, and in their own country they are laying the foundations for a type of architecture that is more in tune with the new social needs.'

Jürgen Joedicke wrote in his 'Geschichte der modernen Architektur' (The History of Modern Architecture), published by Verlag Arthur Niggli, Teufen, Switzerland, 1958: 'During and after World War II a feeling of uncertainty pervades Dutch architecture. Even architects like J. J. P. Oud fail to recapture the clear lines of their former work. This decline can probably be ascribed to the small country's isolation in a Europe devastated by war, the lack of contact with the centres of modern architecture, which had moved to the United States, and to the enormous material and economic damage wrought in the country.

It was not until about 1948 that a start was made with large-scale reconstruction work in the devastated areas. More than a quarter of the dwellings had been destroyed or damaged as a result of the war. The housing shortage was aggravated by the rising birthrate, which was already high compared with that of neighbouring countries. House-building was therefore the principal task, and some excellent results were achieved, for example, in the Amsterdam district of Frankendaal (1949–1951), built by the architects Merkelbach and Elling.

The reconstruction of the centre of Rotterdam, which had been completely destroyed, offered an excellent opportunity for putting new ideas into practice. Co-operation between artisans and small industries resulted in the construction of multi-purpose buildings, smaller or larger units of which could be rented as workshops and offices and all the necessary connections for electricity, gas and water were provided. The focal point of Rotterdam's reconstruction is the 'Lijnbaan' shopping centre, which is reserved for pedestrians only. It was designed by the Dutch architects J. H. van den Broek and J. B. Bakema, who have thereby raised the reputation of Dutch architecture abroad once more. The expression of form in their work, reminiscent of the heyday of Dutch architecture between 1917 and 1938, does not neglect attention to detail; it is severe and arresting without being bold, for it is based on the carefully thought-out juxtaposition of different materials. Their buildings (department store in Rotterdam, 1949–1950, offices and warehouses of Van Houten in Rotterdam, 1952) demonstrate the strength of modern design based on simple stereometric forms'.

G. E. Kidder Smith, like the German writers already quoted, is of the opinion that there was a decline in Dutch architecture after the war. In his architectural guide 'The New Architecture of Europe' (The World Publishing Company, Cleveland and New York, 1961) he, too, praises the 'Lijnbaan' shopping centre and Aldo van Eyck's Amsterdam Orphanage, but expresses the opinion that Oud has 'apparently deliberately confused the forms' in his Second Liberal Reformed 'Lycée' in The Hague.

He condemns the 'Grote Schouwburg' (Theatre) in Rotterdam, the new railway stations in Flushing and Bois-le-Duc and the 'Provinciehuis' (Provincial Building) in Arnhem as 'Continental horrors', and believes many people share his opinion. The architecture of the Church of the Good Shepherd in Oosterbeek-Hoog by F. A. Eschauzier, the 'neo-romantic' Church of the Cross in Amstelveen by M. F. Duintjer, the Maranatha Church in Amsterdam-South by Groenewegen and Mieras and the Reformed Church in Schiedam by J. H. van den Broek and J. B. Bakema, he considers good. He also expresses admiration for the interior of Oud's 'Lycée' already mentioned, although he dislikes the building as a whole, and for the interior of the Montessori 'Lycée' in Rotterdam by Van den Broek and Bakema, of which he says that 'it is a good piece of work, but rather raw.'

One may not always wholly agree with those opinions, but it is evident that the writers are fairly well informed and that their general impressions correspond on the whole with the views of the majority of Dutch architects themselves. It should, however, be realized that both in architecture and in town planning the opportunities have not only multiplied, but the needs have also changed to such a degree that it is more than ever a case of 'Anything is acceptable, provided it is good'. This is no doubt a very vague guiding principle, but it is none the less the accepted principle in present-day architecture both at home and abroad, and it is after all not so difficult to pick out what is good. In a lecture he gave in March 1961, W. van Tijen presented the other side of the national and international picture. He said:

'Architecture does not consist solely of designers and buildings; mentality and custom also come into it. I should like to say something more about them because they influence architecture to such a great extent. I believe that, especially since the last war, several utterly wrong practices have crept into our architecture. The trouble lies with the great men in our profession. Granpré Molière introduced the architect-philosopher and Le Corbusier the architect-visionary, orator, prophet and all that. The novel, 'The Fountainhead', with its ridiculous character of Roark, who ravished the woman he loved and married her to his arch-enemy to prove his love, and blew up his skyscraper because he did not quite like a balcony, was perhaps the last straw.

And so we now have been saddled with the architect-hero, the architect-orator, the architect-prophet, the architect-martyr, the architect-world-reformer. You are no architect unless you possess at least several of those attributes.

This lies at the root of a great many unfortunate practices. The endless rhetorical and vague utterances of so many architects, the enormously inflated ideas of their own work that they have, the way they over-advertise it at home and abroad – to mention only the village of Nagele – the monopolization of architecture and town planning by men of limited vision – these are all signs of one-sidedness and immaturity, confusing to the younger generation, and liable to hold back vital new trends in architecture. Today's 'Forum' (the years 1959, 1960, 1961 and 1962, of the 'Forum' magazine were discussed the evening this address was delivered) can hardly be said to counter those tendencies.

I would draw your attention especially to the lack of self-criticism. Every self-respecting architect nowadays believes that he must and does create nothing but masterpieces. That is preposterous. Every book of poetry, including those of the greatest poets, proves incontestably that only very few poems are of lasting merit.

The same can be said of the work of the best, even of the most outstanding architects (take Wright, for instance); only a small part of what they have built will stand the test of time.

This does not alter the fact that, every time an architect starts a new project, his purpose should be to tackle some essential aspect of the building problem. He should be satisfied with succeeding only partly almost every time, and as long as his intentions are good, he has nothing to be ashamed of. Even the best and the most conscientious architect will only very occasionally, and then perhaps to his own and everybody else's surprise, succeed in creating something great that can be considered to be a valuable and permanent contribution to architecture. If he succeeds in doing that, he may well be proud and particularly grateful; he cannot count on an unbroken run of success.

It would be wrong and harmful to the development of architecture, however, to pretend to oneself and to others that one's failures are really superior creations, the worth of which is not yet understood. This method, to which unfortunately even the best architects are sometimes not averse, (Le Corbusier and the fiasco of his pavilion in Brussels), is most confusing, especially to the younger generation'.

It is evident from such personal outpourings emanating from one of the leading modern architects, and a member of the former C.I.A.M. group that, here too, there is great diversity of opinion, for Van Tijen's criticisms were levelled at an editorial staff of which J. B. Bakema and Aldo van Eyck, also former members of the C.I.A.M. group, were members.

These 'younger' architects, who ran the 'Forum' magazine, (between 1959 and 1962), were opposing the threat of mechanization, especially in house-building, and the domination of building by technicians, demographers and other 'scientific' town planners, in short, all influences outside the architectural profession. Despite their strained style and excited statements, sometimes full of self-glorification, they showed themselves genuinely concerned about the way in which people were being packed together in 'glorified' warehouses. Expressions like the following could certainly not be misinterpreted: 'First and foremost, two facts should be put on record. The first – that Holland is so overcrowded that it is becoming uninhabitable – is a reality that one becomes aware of as one gets shorter of breath. The second – that both architects and town planners, whose existences and reason for existence should be based on their having imagination and the ability to create form and on their using those powers, are largely responsible for making this small country uninhabitable – is so paradoxical that it is at least beginning to weigh on the conscience.' ('Forum' No. 7 of 1959). In the same issue, the architects were again claiming the right to act as town planners, using the statements made by Smithsons and Howell, members of Commission 6 at the C.I.A.M. Congress in Aix-en-Provence in 1952, to support their arguments. Smithsons and Howell said: 'Housing and town planning lie in the same field of activity. The 'town planner' is an unrealistic invention of the twenties resulting from circumstances and the one-sidedness of the architect. The town planner, like a physician, made his diagnoses of the diseases from which the big towns suffered and prescribed his medicines, without realizing that an organism might be cured, but not created, by administering medicines. *A town is not cured, it is given new life.* It is difficult to get a town planner away from academic abstract planning based on forms that are already there, instead of on forms that do not yet exist. It is, after all, impossible to put a tree together, even if the parts are made of wood. They would not be real branches and so would not be able to produce any leaves.' (Page 220 of 'Forum' No. 7 of 1959). The editors contrasted the Arabian Casbah with the monotony of system-built blocks of flats and the bareness of many neighbourhoods planned with too much open space; they advocated what might be called 'enclosure' instead of 'openness', 'care' instead of speed and indifference to intimacy and comfort. There was no end to their theorizing. Examples can demonstrate better than words what the editors of 'Forum' meant. There are, for instance, the dwellings in 'Spangen', Rotterdam, designed by Michiel Brinkman in 1919, the designs submitted by Walter Schwagenscheidt and Tassilo Sittman for the E.C.S.C. prize in 1959, P. Blom's town-planning projects, and Schindler's work in Los Angeles during the 'twenties. (When Bakema was appointed Professor of Architecture at the Institute of Advanced Technology at Delft, he said during his inaugural address: 'The origin of the residential areas in which we live today can often be traced to the fact that it was decided at the last moment, because of a change in financial policy, to substitute a different type of housing for the one that had been carefully designed in relation to the general lay-out and the surroundings, without, however, making the necessary adjustments in the basic plan because, for example, the streets had already been built and the mains laid. In this way one of the most important functions of planning is completely ignored, which the Californian architect Schindler explains as follows in 'The Contemporary House' (probably in 1940): '... the planner-architect views the house or the whole town as the expression of one cosmic space. The house becomes an organism in which all the rooms are interrelated variations of one basic scheme. The house becomes a fabric of a few fundamental materials which are used to fix physical forms in space ...') Other examples illustrating what the editors of 'Forum' mean are the designs of 'younger' architects like Koning, Tupker, Stroeve, Manten and Van Stigt. Their ideas met with great response among the younger generation, although it was of course evident to many that architecture and town planning were being 'reunited' in the Netherlands as in other parts of the world. More and bigger shopping centres, which are typical examples of that reunion, were being built in this country.

In this connection it is very instructive to read what B. Merkelbach says in an article which appeared in the magazine 'De 8 en Opbouw' (Volume 3, number 1 of 7th January 1932). He wrote: 'A great many houses have been built in the last few years. In Amsterdam, for instance, whole new districts have sprung up; a sea of houses surrounds the old city. Amsterdam has always been a great city, so when it started to build houses, not only was that done on a large scale, but the authorities also had a say in the matter. Houses were not allowed to be built 'anyhow'; no, everything was nicely 'arranged'. Commissions were set up, architects covered countless sheets of paper with their designs, building companies were formed (some of which went bankrupt), everyone and everything was drawn into the business of building houses.'

'High houses, low houses, round houses, square houses, houses without towers, houses with towers, houses with balconies, houses without balconies, houses with living rooms facing East, West, South or North, houses with gardens, houses without gardens – everything arranged strictly in accordance with the ideas of the Commissions'.

'The unsuspecting visitor may think that there are people actually living in all those houses, but he will be mistaken. It is true that they are all occupied by people who are trying to live there, but there is no question of LIVING in the real sense. Why ever not? Well, the simple explanation is that the houses have not been built to be LIVED in. It is true that great pains have been taken to design attractive façades, there are all kinds of windows in every imaginable shape as evidence that no trouble or expense has been spared, but if you were to ask whether the most rudimentary requirements of living comfort have been taken into account, our reply would have to be: NO, in no way whatsoever!

The Amsterdamer, good-natured creature that he is, makes the best of camping in those houses.'

Merkelbach then lists the inadequacies of the houses built in the 'thirties, spicing his remarks with humour, laying particular emphasis on the unacceptable ground-plans and the technical shortcomings. Much has changed since then, but the advances made are smaller than had been hoped and anticipated. If, therefore, a comparison is made between the ideas of the C.I.A.M. group and those of the 'younger' architects (Bakema and Van Eyck belonged to the so-called X Team, whose aim it was to carry on and to develop the ideas of the C.I.A.M. group) it would be more correct to say that there was a difference in 'interpretation' rather than in attitude or outlook, for the former C.I.A.M. members could to some extent still be considered to be advocates of functionalism, though they were drifting further apart.

However, if one cares to take the trouble, it is still possible to distinguish three separate groups, but the former C.I.A.M. group and the 'younger' architects who feel an affinity with it must then be split up into groups which, to an even greater extent than the old C.I.A.M. members, are 'groping' for a form instead of distilling it from their commissions as the C.I.A.M. adherents had to do.

This is a question of emphasis rather than principle, although if the 'function of the form' is recognized, a 'new' element is introduced into the creative function. It should then be realized that too much emphasis on this 'function of form' might lead to a new kind of 'art for art's sake'.

If it can be assumed, as it can in the Netherlands, that the former members of the C.I.A.M. who still subscribe to the principles of that group are, in fact, not so far removed from the 'younger' architects, (who, despite a certain urge to find their own form, certainly have no wish to conform to the views of the more modern '1932 Group',) one would still have to regard these generally progressive and internationally minded architects as a single group – making allowances, of course, for typically Dutch characteristics arising from the use of bricks, the type of soil, the climate and the composition of the population. One still comes across the dogmatic traditionalists, but their number and influence are fast diminishing. Finally, the great majority of Dutch architects can be included in a large middle group which wants to be modern without repudiating tradition, or wants to remain traditional and yet follow contemporary fashion in architecture. This modern eclecticism prevails widely and one of its most obvious characteristics is the excessive and often ridiculous use of glass, especially for office buildings, some of which are little more than glass boxes built over concrete frames. Moreover, in the last few years a 'Stijl' fashion has emerged that involves the indiscriminate employment of the primary colours Mondriaan used, viz. red, yellow and blue, for both the exterior and the interior decoration of new buildings. Those who are following it are no less guilty of eclecticism than the people who are trying to imitate functionalism now that that is becoming the fashion again in this country as in others. These half-baked architects, who are incapable of designing anything genuinely functional, hide themselves in the middle group among those who reject on principle a too universally applied matter-of-factness. They are in the first place the functional traditionalists, the former '1932 Group', which included Arthur Staal, Boeken, Komter, Giesen, Sijmons, Duintjer, Van Woerden and Zanstra. In the same group are architects who were originally and 'by nature' traditionalistically inclined, but who have now, not unsuccessfully, discarded the old forms and adopted a fairly individualistic modernism. Many of them are ex-pupils of Professor Granpré Molière of Delft, who, like Berlage, has produced a few recalcitrant, or in this case rather 'moderately' recalcitrant, followers. Among these formerly traditionalistic and now relatively modern architects are Holt, Vegter, Peutz (who is sometimes surprisingly modern, even in his earlier work, which includes the House of Retreat and a department store at Heerlen), Zwiers, Berghoef (who is responsible for some good dwellings but also for several unsatisfactory town halls), Van Embden (who designed the Institutes of Advanced Technology at Eindhoven and Enschede, the latter in collaboration with Van Tijen), and Van den Erve. These architects are all equally able, although some are more 'modernistic' than others.

Among the traditionalists one finds many semi-qualified builders and contractors who work to their own designs, which are only just within the limits of what is considered acceptable. These people, who are unfortunately free to do as they like in the Netherlands where the profession of architect has not yet been accorded legal status, naturally avoid new forms and are quite content to imitate the work of the traditionalists.

The ignorance of these people is responsible for the great number of unimaginative new dwellings in villages and small towns. Granpré Molière and his pupils or followers, such as Pouderoyen, De Bruyn, Nix, Kuiper, Gouwetor, De Ranitz, Treep, Evers and Sarlemijn are among the serious and able architects in this group. However, their work is often so out-of-date that it can hardly be said to have a place in present-day society.

Among the C.I.A.M. group of architects there were also a few who more or less blindly copied the external features of the 'international style'. However, as the members of the group were very critical of each other's work, the general level was fairly high. There was a danger, however, that outside the group the trend would be towards a style which was derived largely from foreign sources and which I should like to term 'eclectical modern'. A lone figure is S. van Ravesteijn, who was originally allied to the C.I.A.M. group, but later went his own wilful way and developed a new baroque style. His work is particularly remarkable in that it has always been strongly individualistic, even when he was groping towards a personal style in the face of opposition from the group to which he had once belonged.

The orthodox modern architects, the former C.I.A.M. group, were placed in a very difficult position, as the whole world sat in judgment on their work, criticizing it far more severely than that of other architects. Were they making a positive contribution to the development of a new style or was their work imitative? Before World War II it was Oud's 'Kiefhoek', the Open Air School, and the Van Nelle factory, that opened up new architectural perspectives. It is difficult to tell at this stage whether the work of the leading members of this group has reached the exceptionally high standard of the buildings referred to above, but there is no doubt that the general level of Dutch architecture today is judged mainly on the merits of their work. Apart from a few arch-traditionalists, not a single architect who has accepted the new technical processes and the new attitude to living that was emerging has failed to be influenced by them, but, owing to an incomprehensible conservatism, the number of commissions they received both before and after the war was not commensurate with their ability. The functionalists in this country remained true to their principles and, with the exception of Van den Broek, Bakema and Van Eyck, did not succeed in finding a point of departure that would have enabled them to acquire greater freedom. Oud and Rietveld remained free, but such opportunities as they were given came too late. Oud, who always kept aloof from every group and who occasionally refused commissions he did not care for, was not greatly in demand immediately after the war, but just before his death in 1963 he was engaged on several big projects. With the Second Liberal Reformed 'Lycée' in The Hague, Oud showed that an obstinately determined man is always proved right in the end. At first sight his ground-plan of a main building with a separate gymnasium looks simple enough; but it is in fact a happy medium between functionalism and the monumental saved from triviality by Oud's sense of proportion. Yet it is remarkable that traces of both 'De Stijl' and the Amsterdam School can be detected in this work. When building the Bio Children's Holiday Centre near Arnhem he was prompted by a strong desire to create a new form, with the result that he made the caretaker's lodge and the adjacent boiler-house the focal point of the complex of buildings. He also failed to make full use of the beautiful surroundings when designing the nurses' home.

Rietveld, whose untimely death in 1964 deprived Dutch architects of his example and his mild yet shrewd judgement at a time when they would greatly have benefited by them, was given few big commissions. Although this gave him little opportunity to develop his talents, it did not prevent him from producing small masterpieces, like the 'Biennale' pavilion in Venice, a small exhibition building in Amersfoort, offices in Zwolle and a pavilion for objects of sculptural art in Arnhem (since 1965 in Otterlo). After his seventieth year he was suddenly rediscovered and received several larger commissions, including those for Industrial Arts Training Centres in Amsterdam and Arnhem. He can really be considered a universally recognized master who has always held his own.

Merkelbach, who went into partnership with Elling after World War II but gave up his private practice after being appointed city architect of Amsterdam in 1957, designed a number of industrial buildings for Beynes, Ketjen and Tetterode, all of which are businesslike, very severe, completely straightforward and without the slightest suggestion of compromise, notwithstanding the fact that he was an almost 'classic' negotiator, leader of discussions and arbiter.

When the partnership with Elling came to an end, Merkelbach undertook to complete the 'GAK' Office in Amsterdam, which, although it was jointly designed by both architects, in my opinion very clearly betrays Merkelbach's style. It is a particularly plain building, which, in fact, excels only because of its perfect proportions. Though simple at first sight, the longer and more closely one looks at it, the more impressive it becomes.

Merkelbach, who was one of the leading members of the former C.I.A.M. group, has not derived much satisfaction from his position as city architect. He was given little opportunity to do any really creative work, and since there are so few architects in this country who are capable of tackling large projects with any measure of success, this was most regrettable. Merkelbach was one of the most important architects in the Netherlands, the leading figure of the 'second generation' after Oud and Rietveld; his death in 1961 meant the end of the C.I.A.M., which had, in fact, been disbanded as early as 1956, the end of a group which, ever since 1930, had more or less successfully opposed the stubborn humdrum middle-class ideas of many short-sighted principals, inspired as it was by an unquenchable love of architecture and a great sense of social responsibility. Merkelbach was one of the 'new men' of architecture of whom Rietveld had been one of the first in the Netherlands, with Van Eyck and Bakema carrying on the tradition; he was a man for whom architecture was the means of giving his fellow men what they deserved and needed in their homes and in their offices or factories, in social intercourse and recreation. He believed, and rightly so, that architecture should not only indicate new trends but also serve a practical purpose, and that it is the needs of people, who, after all, constitute society, that determine the function and the form or construction of every building from beginning to end.

Maaskant, an 'easy' but talented architect, also built factories, flats and multi-purpose buildings, sometimes in collaboration with Van Tijen. The latter, however, specialized more in houses and town planning and has designed several districts, especially those in Vlaardingen, which are among the most successful in the whole of the Netherlands. Maaskant and Van Tijen parted company in

1956; they both went into partnership with a number of younger architects, Van Tijen with Boom and Posno, Maaskant with Van Dommelen, Senf and Kroos. Groosman, like Romke de Vries, is talented; both have taste and know how to use modern forms attractively. Elling was primarily a designer of villas, but later, when he collaborated with Merkelbach, he proved that he was capable of designing on a larger scale. He had a very personal style, often extremely sober, which explains why he and Merkelbach suited each other. After the partnership was dissolved, he steadily improved his style, but unfortunately died in 1962 before he was able to complete a number of big projects.

Salomonson, who also specializes in villas, has always produced good work. Jan Rietveld is best known for his villas, too. Bijvoet, who first collaborated with Duiker, later designed a few good, small theatres together with Holt. Kloos built several orthodox hospitals and schools; Haan some attractive villas. There are also a number of younger architects, such as Boon, Van Stigt, Blom, Jelles, Bekink, André de Jong, Römelingh, and of course many others who have not yet made a name for themselves. Most of the really big commissions were unfortunately entrusted to lesser architects. There are, after all, more of them and they are usually more tractable.

These 'lesser' architects are, however, largely responsible for establishing the standard of Dutch architecture and the picture presented by the country as a whole. Though their names are not very well known, they must, however, be counted among the able architects. It is easy to draw up a list of thirty such architects whose names have not yet been mentioned, but that list would still be incomplete: Boks, Knijtijzer, Boosten, Brouwer, Deurvorst, Klarenbeek, Greiner, Van der Gaast, Van der Grinten, Spruit, Cuypers, Nicolaï, Slebos, Dijkstra, Ingwersen, Fledderus, Klein, Lucas, Olsmeyer, Pennink, Mastenbroek, Abma, Pot, Pot-Keegstra, Nix and Starmans. For further information the list of buildings after 1945, given on the last page of this book, should be consulted. They include old and young, some on the threshold of their careers, others in middle life, with few opportunities for further development. But let us make no mistake; foreign experts view Dutch architecture as a whole, and it is the architects mentioned above, and scores of others who have not been named, who are jointly responsible for the impression created outside the country. The few outstanding buildings will undoubtedly be discussed in foreign publications, but they hardly affect the general level.

It is the standard of the 'average' architect, that of the 'average' production which is below par. There are too many unqualified and partially qualified people, too many 'passengers' and imitators, too many obstinate old gentlemen who abhor 'the modern trend', who clutter up the towns and the countryside with the abortive and unworthy products of their minds. If only we had achieved a higher average, an average that would in all probability have been despised by revolutionaries like Bakema and Van Eyck, but which would nevertheless have been gratifying if it could be seen all over the country.

Bakema and Van Eyck are undoubtedly the most obsessed men in the Dutch architectural world; they are different in temperament but similar in their despair and in their enthusiasm. They are both in their early forties, belong to the 'third' generation after Oud and Rietveld and strongly oppose the 'second generation' of Merkelbach, Kloos and Van Tijen; they are well-informed about what is happening in other countries, and they are firmly resolved to find their own style, which is neither international nor typically Dutch, but first and foremost typically either Bakema or Van Eyck.

When comparing Dutch architecture with the latest architectural developments abroad, the following may be noted. It is a well-known fact that functionalism has been identified with skeleton construction for a long time. In this type of building the framework may be outwardly visible or not and mathematical rectangular forms, straight lines and flat surfaces are preferred. But since the twenties, the shell roof construction has also been developed in which, as Gropius says, the roof is really the actual building. This type of construction allows more freedom in the choice of form. Although the 'old' functionalism is now gradually coming to the fore in the Netherlands, sometimes mixed with traditional ideas, sometimes purely eclectic, there are no signs yet in this country that much thought is being given to the finding of such forms as have been made possible by the shell roof construction. We have already mentioned that building is generally on a small scale in the Netherlands and this may explain the lack of interest in structural innovations. On the other hand, the number of industrial buildings and congress and exhibition halls erected during the last few years should have been an inducement to make a closer study of new construction methods and to try to translate the new technical inventions into new architectural forms.

It is strange that there are no traces whatsoever in the Netherlands of the constructionist movement, which dates back to Maillart or even earlier to the beginning of the nineteenth century, starting perhaps with Telford and carried on by Nervi, Candela and Torroja, or of Novicki's method of hanging roofs and the experiments of Buckminster, Fuller and Wachsmann. Nor has there been any attempt to find new architectural forms which would more or less result from the above-mentioned 'method', derived from construction, and which lead to work like that of Eero Saarinen, Jörn Utzon, Castiglioni and others. Perhaps the Dutch found this shell or whelk style too dangerous, seeing that the shock they had received from the excesses of the Amsterdam School was still fresh in their minds; for the Amsterdam School had produced similar forms, albeit not from considerations of construction.

It is nevertheless strange that little attention is being paid in the Netherlands to the expressionism of the later Scharoun, the closed-in-ness of Kahn, the use of glass behind the concrete frame, which was probably introduced by Gropius in his embassy building in Athens (and used later by others, including Abramovitz and Ralph Rapson, by the latter very decoratively), or to the Japanese and the 'American' Japanese. If it is borne in mind, however, that both Berlage and the 'Stijl' Group were fascinated by the problem of relating architectural form to space, especially in respect of walls, it is somewhat surprising that this 'tradition' has hardly taken root in the Netherlands and that, at any rate in the designs of buildings already completed, little or no account has been taken of the problems arising from the tendency to make a building a single work of plastic art, as Le Corbusier had done with his chapel at Ronchamp, or, in another way, Paul Rudolph with his building for art and architecture of Yale University, or, in yet another way, Walter Förderer, Rolf Otto and Hans Zwimpfer with their schools at Aesch near Basle and St. Gallen. It is easy to understand that this leads to the integration of plastic art and architecture, the first being merged into the second, a development which Berlage must have had in mind when he wished to subordinate the plastic arts to architecture in his conception of 'total architecture': '. . . for sculptors and painters should realize that the greatest strength of their art lies in its relation to architecture. It is true that it is possible for sculpture and painting to develop separately, depending on the purpose for which they are intended, but if, as in the past, architecture is again to make use of the two 'sister' arts in its own sphere, it is essential that co-ordination of style be re-established. And in naturalism there was no question of co-ordination of style, because the form of expression in the arts of painting and sculpture was based on differing interpretations of nature'. (H. P. Berlage's 'Schoonheid in Samenleving' (Beauty in Society), on page 116 of the chapter 'De bouwkunst als maatschappelijke kunst' (Architecture as a social art)).

There are few architects in the Netherlands who enliven their architectural theme in concrete, stone or brick with the aid of the plastic arts, independently or assisted by sculptors or painters, although it is true that brickwork is the traditional material used for modest decoration.

The tendency is towards dissociating the plastic arts from architecture rather than integrating the two, and it is equal worth rather than co-ordination of style which makes it possible for them to exist in harmony with one another. Good examples of this harmony are the paintings by Appel and the architecture of J. J. P. Oud in the Second Liberal Reformed 'Lycée' in The Hague, Couzijn's sculpture in front of the Unilever building in Rotterdam, Gabo's sculpture in front of 'De Bijenkorf' building by Elzas and Breuer in Rotterdam, and a pavilion of sculptures in front of an office building by Merkelbach and Elling in Amsterdam. However, such examples are also to be found outside the Netherlands and they are by no means typical examples of the integration or even of attempts at the integration of the plastic arts and architecture. Moreover, the need to make architecture independent of the plastic arts by incorporating all elements thereof is simply not felt.

Other experiments, too, such as those of Frank Lloyd Wright in his later years, of Gardella, or the 'new brutalism' of the Smithsons, have found and are still finding little response in the Netherlands, with the exception of a few, often anything but successful, details. Although all these experiments can certainly lead to confusion, it appears that architecture can develop in the same way as painting did in the first half of this century, with an abundance of -isms. It has been realized in other countries, and is gradually being realized in the Netherlands, too, that what we call architecture cannot be embodied in theories any more than literature can. The standard is established by what is actually built, thus by the architects themselves, and not by the theoreticians, or members of the older generation, who have sometimes acquired fixed ideas, which helped to dispose of the eclecticism of the nineteenth century in the past but which, in the shape of new dogmas, could now hamper new developments. This does not mean that the 'old' functionalism cannot be developed further in the future, though there would then be a risk of creating a new kind of eclecticism, as is sometimes evident, especially in the Netherlands, from the work of 'converted' traditionalists.

Is the Netherlands not going to participate in international developments? If the technical aids were to remain unchanged, it might be predicted, as for the plastic arts, that a contemporary Dutch architect will be able to cut across all these trends and movements and find his own form for what he wants to express. It is possible that we are on the brink of an era of consolidation conducive to the creation of 'masterpieces' in the sense that they are personal and do not permit of a further development.

It is not possible to compare architecture and the plastic arts fully for several reasons. Architecture, like science, must always be 'open' to new technical inventions, which may change its character completely, and, in contrast to science, must be even 'more open' to social changes. Above all, it should be 'most open' to the fact that architecture and town planning may be integrated to such an extent that there can no longer be any question of an individual work of art.

Architecture has always been and still is an applied art, but it has at the same time been given unprecedented opportunities which are determined and prescribed by social developments. It would be foolish to suppose that there are not many architects in the Netherlands who realize what 'applied opportunities' there are in architecture today. They should endeavour to create 'preliminary masterpieces', in the sense that they should do their utmost to realize their own personal ideas. That is, expressed as simply as possibly: the synthesis, the personal synthesis of all that has been achieved in the past fifty years, simply, light-heartedly and freely making use of any 'personal' idea of any other architect (thus quite contrary to the personality cult of Le Corbusier, who claims certain architectural innovations for himself, an originality-fetishism rampant among us today, which has never before been experienced in architecture because it has always been an art in which experiences were pooled), a synthesis that is also directed to other fields quite different from architecture, as unbiased as possible (thus almost in the manner of Rietveld) in wishing to give people what they may expect from architecture but what cannot be expressed in words.

*Dr. H. P. Berlage* – Stock Exchange, Damrak, Amsterdam, 1897–1903

↑ *W. M. Dudok* – Snellius School, Hilversum, 1931

← *M. de Klerk* – Houses, Henriëtte Ronnerplein, Amsterdam, 1921

*Dr. J. J. P. Oud* – 'Kiefhoek' residential area, Rotterdam, 1925

*G. T. Rietveld* – The Schröder residence, Utrecht, 1924

*J. A. Brinkman and L. C. van der Vlugt* – Van Nelle factory, Rotterdam, 1928

*J. Duiker* – Cinema, Reguliersbreestraat, Amsterdam, 1936

*De Ruyter and v. d. Graaf* – Warehouse, Rijnhaven, Rotterdam, 1949

*G. C. Bremer* – Railway post-office, The Hague, 1948

Aldo van Eijck – Children's playground, Dijkstraat, Amsterdam, 1954.
B. Merkelbach and P. Elling, Lettergieterij "Amsterdam" formerly N. Tetterode N.V. (Type Foundry),
Amsterdam, 1950

↑ *W. van Tijen and H. A. Maaskant* – Wholesale Trade Building. Rotterdam. Goods are despatched from various floors, 1948–1951

← *M. F. Duintjer* – Protestant church, Charlotte van Montpensierlaan, Amstelveen, 1953

Prof. J. H. van den Broek and Prof. J. B. Bakema – 'Lijnbaan' shopping-centre, Rotterdam, 1953

H. A. Maaskant – 'Nederland-Kattenburg' clothing store, Beursplein, Rotterdam, 1952

K. L. *Sijmons* – Protestant church, Hengelolaan, The Hague, 1955

G. T. *Rietveld* – Pavilion for plastic art exhibitions, Sonsbeek Park, 1954–55, since 1965 in the National Park "De Hoge Veluwe" at Otterlo

← *J. W. C. Boks* – International Information Centre for Building and Housing, Weena, Rotterdam, 1948 and 1955

↓ *Prof. J. H. van den Broek and Prof. J. B. Bakema* – Department store, Hoogstraat, Rotterdam, 1956

← *Amsterdam Public Works Office (D. Slebos)* – Tramways control tower, Stationsplein, Amsterdam 1955

↓ *Prof. J. H. van den Broek and Prof. J. B. Bakema* – Doctor's residence, Middelharnis, 1957

← *E. F. Groosman* – Dwellings, Herdersplein, Utrecht, 1955

↓ *G. J. van der Grinten* – Railway station, Den Helder, 1958

←  *Dudok Architectural Bureau (W. M. Dudok and R. M. H. Magnée)* – Port of Amsterdam Authority office building, Amsterdam, 1958–60

↓  *Hein Salomonson* – House, Apollolaan, Amsterdam, 1960

*Aldo van Eijck* – Orphanage, Amstelveense Weg, Amsterdam, 1960

*Van Tijen, Boom and Posno Architecture and Town Planning Group (M. Boom)* – Agricultural Research
Building, Wageningen, 1961

*Prof. J. H. van den Broek and Prof. J. B. Bakema* – Protestant church, Nagele, 1960–61

*Prof. J. H. van den Broek and Prof. J. B. Bakema* – Church precinct and playground for the infant school run by the Dutch Reformed Church, Nagele, 1960–61

*Prof. P. Elling* – Industries Fair Office, Vreeburg, Utrecht, 1962

*H. A. Maaskant* – 'Tomado' office building, Stationsplein, Dordrecht, 1960–62

*B. Bijvoet and Prof. G. H. M. Holt* – Theatre, Tilburg, 1961

*A. J. N. Boosten* – Roman Catholic church, Walramplein, Valkenburg, 1961

*G. T. Rietveld* – Fine Arts Academy, Onderlangs, Arnhem, 1962

*D. van Mourik and J. W. du Pon* – I.B.M. laboratory, Uithoorn, 1963

*Merkelbach and Elling Architectural Bureau (B. Merkelbach and A. Bodon)* – Gemeenschappelijk Administratiekantoor (Mutual Administration Office), Amsterdam, 1957–60

*Merkelbach and Elling Architectural Bureau (B. Merkelbach and A. Bodon)* – Sculptures, Gemeenschappe-lijk Administratiekantoor (Mutual Administration Office), Amsterdam, 1964

← *Wessel Couzijn* – 'Unity Embodied', sculpture in front of the Unilever Building, Burgemeester 's Jacobplein, Rotterdam, 1963

↓ *Prof. S. J. van Embden Architectural Bureau* – Institute of Advanced Technology, Eindhoven, 1960 and later

*J. van Stigt* – Staff canteen, Institute of Advanced Technology, Enschede, 1964

# List of buildings

## AALSMEER

Boiler-house, 27 Hornweg. *Prof. J. F. Berghoef*, 1948.

Leyland-Holland car factory, Provincialeweg/Zwarteweg. *J. Brouwer*, 1956.

Houses, 24 Hornweg, 164 Kudelstaartseweg, 104 Stommerweg, 17a Zwarteweg. *Prof. J. F. Berghoef and H. Klarenbeek*, 1957–1958.

"Bloemenlust", Co-operative auction society, extension. *Prof. J. F. Berghoef and H. Klarenbeek*, 1959 onwards.

## AERDENHOUT

Villa, 1a Zwarteweg. *B. Bijvoet and Prof. G. H. M. Holt*, 1951.

Protestant church, Leeuwerikenlaan. *K. L. Sijmons*, 1958.

Heemstede-Aerdenhout railway station. *K. van der Gaast*, 1958.

Villa, Boekenrodeweg. *H. van Leeuwen*, 1960.

## ALKMAAR

'Don Bosco' Roman Catholic Church, Geert Groteplein. *Prof. A. van Kranendonk and J. Lochtenberg*, 1961.

Wholesale premises and factory, 86–88 Luttik Oudorp. *C. Kirkenier and P. Selle*, 1961.

## ALMELO

'De Klokkenbelt' Home for the Aged, Vriessenveenseweg. *A. Komter*, 1951.

Princess Irene Hospital, Verlengde Hofkampstraat. *J. P. Kloos, M. Baereveldt, O. Greiner and K. F. G. Spruit*, 1959.

Post-office. *J. B. Koning and J. C. Rentjes*, 1960 onwards.

Town hall. *Dr. J. J. P. Oud*, 1963 onwards.

Railway Station. *K. van der Gaast*, 1963.

## ALPHEN a/d RIJN

Factory, van Foreestlaan/Energieweg. *J. Visser*, 1959.

Printing offices, van Foreestlaan/Prinses Margrietlaan. *Maaskant, Van Dommelen, Kroos and Senf*, 1960.

## AMERSFOORT

Flats and houses, Soesterkwartier. *D. Zuiderhoek*, 1947–1956.

School, Bosweg. *D. Zuiderhoek*, 1954.

School, Kruiskamp. *D. Zuiderhoek*, 1954.

Flats, Randenbroek. *D. Zuiderhoek*, 1955.

Houses, Kapelweg. *D. Zuiderhoek*, 1955.

Infant school, Kruiskamp. *D. Zuiderhoek*, 1956.

Infant school, Lambert Heinrichstraat.
*D. Zuiderhoek*, 1956.

Hospital, Laan 1914. *L. H. P. Waterman*, 1957.

'Evert Kupersoord', holiday and study centre, 9 Laan 1914. *H. W. Brakel and W. Buma*, 1958.

Roman Catholic church, De Ruyterstraat. *C. J. van Wissen*, 1959.

'Zonnehof' Cultureel Centrum (cultural centre), near Utrechtseweg. *G. T. Rietveld*, 1960.

Savings bank, Snouckaertlaan/Utrechtseweg. *J. H. Oosterhuis*, 1960.

Protestant church, 74 Kruiskamp. *T. van Hoogevest*, 1962.

AMSTELVEEN

Protestant church, Charlotte de Montpensier-laan. *Prof. M. F. Duintjer*, 1953.

Van Leer's Vatenfabriek N.V. (barrel factory) office building and canteen, 206 Amsterdamseweg. *Marcel Breuer*, 1958.

Villa, 4 Prinses Marijkelaan. *F. U. Verbruggen and P. R. Goldschmidt*, 1958.

Amsterdam-Rotterdam Bank N.V. Centrumplein. *Arthur Staal*, 1959.

Blocks of flats with external galleries, maisonettes and houses for the aged, Keizer Karel Park. *D. Zuiderhoek*, 1959.

Shopping centre. *Prof. J. H. van den Broek and Prof. J. B. Bakema*, 1960-1962.

Various types of flats. *Arthur Staal*, 1960-1963.

West side of shopping centre. *P. Zanstra*, 1960.

Blocks of flats with external galleries, Southwest corner of shopping-centre. *P. Zanstra*, 1961.

Protestant church, Augustinusplantsoen/Lindelaan. *J. B. van Asbeck*, 1962.

AMSTERDAM

National Aeronautical and Astronautical Research Institute, (N.L.R.) 145 Sloterweg. *W. van Tijen and H. A. Maaskant*, 1939 and 1949.

Lettergieterij "Amsterdam", formerly N. Tetterode N.V. (type foundry), Da Costakade. *B. Merkelbach and Prof. P. Elling*, 1950.

Houtveem (timber warehouse), Nieuwe Hemweg. *Office of Public Works*, 1950.

Houses, Hugo de Vrieslaan. *B. Merkelbach and Prof. P. Elling*, 1950.

Koninklijke Zwavelzuurfabriek (sulphuric acid factory) 1-3 Nieuwendammerkade. *B. Merkelbach and Prof. P. Elling*, 1950-1956.

Playgrounds in the old part of the city (before 1940). *Aldo van Eyck*, 1950-1956.

Entrance to 'Werkspoor' canteen, Oostenburgergracht. *Prof. M. F. Duintjer*, 1952.

Houses in the vicinity of Rivierenlaan. *Prof. J. F. Berghoef*, 1952.

Alterations to clothing store, 188-190 Nieuwendijk. *H. Knijtijzer*, 1952.

House, 16 Herman Gorterstraat. *J. Rietveld and Aldo van Eyck*, 1952.

K.L.M. air terminal, Museumplein. *H. Groenewegen*, 1953.

C. & A. clothing store, 197-201 Nieuwendijk. *A. Bodon*, 1953.

Houses for the aged, Jan Bottemastraat. *Aldo van Eyck and J. Rietveld*, 1953.

Houses, Burgemeester de Vlugtlaan. *Prof. J. F. Berghoef*, 1953.

Power station, Nieuwe Hemweg. *Board of Works and Municipal Power Companies*, 1953.

School, Frederiksplein. *H. Knijtijzer*, 1954.

Extension of the Municipal Museum, *Office of Public Works*, 1954.

'Mahez' Building, Buyskade. *B. Merkelbach and Prof. P. Elling*, 1954.

The Amstel Rowing and Yacht Club boathouse, 121-123 Hobbemakade. *Arthur Staal*, 1954.

Shell filling station, 120 Hobbemakade.
*Arthur Staal*, 1954.

Maranatha Church, Hunzestraat, corner of Uiterwaardenstraat. *H. Groenewegen*, 1955.

Houses, De Savornin Lohmanstraat and Confuciusplein. *J. P. Kloos*, 1956.

Confectioners' school, Wibautstraat.
*W. A. Ulrich and B. J. F. Kamphuis*, 1956.

Amsterdam–Sloterdijk railway station.
*K. van der Gaast*, 1956.

Church of the Resurrection (Protestant), Bos en Lommerplein. *Prof. M. F. Duintjer*, 1956.

Shops and houses, Confuciusplein.
*A. Bodon*, 1956.

Protestant church, Surinameplein.
*K. L. Sijmons*, 1956.

'Patrimonium' Technical School, Wibautstraat. *De Geus and J. B. Ingwersen*, 1956.

Baptist church, Burgemeester Rendorpstraat.
*K. L. Sijmons*, 1956.

Youth hostel extension, 32–34 Groenburgwal.
*W. A. Ulrich and B. J. F. Kamphuis*, 1956.

Bakery, Generaal Vetterstraat.
*Joh. A. Riesener and W. Bollebakker*, 1956.

Block of flats with shops, Haarlemmerdijk/
Korte Prinsengracht. *A. Komter*, 1956.

Houses and flats, Beethovenstraat beyond Cornelis Dopperkade. *A. Komter, P. Zanstra, M. Stam, O. Greiner*, 1956.

Houses, Goeman Borgesiusstraat and vicinity, Geuzenveld. *W. M. Dudok*, 1957.

Houses, Sam van Houtenstraat and vicinity, Geuzenveld. *Prof. J. H. van den Broek and Prof. J. B. Bakema*, 1957.

Two blocks of flats with shops, Parnassusweg.
*A. Komter*, 1957.

Zion Calvinist church, 22 Dr. Colijnstraat.
*C. van der Bom*, 1957.

Blocks of flats with external galleries, Burgemeester Cramergracht. *P. Zanstra*, 1957.

Willem Drees Home for the Aged, Hugo de Vrieslaan. *J. A. Snellebrand and G. W. Tuynman*, 1957.

Shops with living accommodation, 250–344 Johan Huizingalaan, Slotervaart.
*F. U. Verbruggen and P. R. Goldschmidt*, 1958.

Bethel Church, (Protestant), Plejadenplein.
*S. van Woerden*, 1958.

'Airey System' Houses, Comeniusstraat, Slotervaart. *Prof. J. F. Berghoef*, 1958–1959.

Honeywell International N.V. 12 Wibautstraat.
*J. A. Riesener and W. Bollebakker*, 1958.

Amsterdamse Ballastmij Office building, Wibautstraat. *Prof. H. T. Zwiers*, 1958.

Houses, 99, 104, and 108 Minervalaan.
*A. Komter* assisted by *L. van Schelt*, 1958.

Factory clinic and radio-chemical laboratory, 3 Badhuisweg. *Arthur Staal* in collaboration with *Shell Building Office*, 1958.

Houses, van Karnebeekstraat and Geuzenveld.
*W. van Tijen*, 1958.

Houses, Plesmanlaan. *E. F. Groosman*, 1958.

'Amatex' office building, 9 Van Riebeekweg.
*J. W. C. Boks, W. Eykelenboom and A. Middelhoek*, 1958.

Bachelor flats, Harry Koningsbergerstraat, Slotermeer. *J. Rietveld and P. R. Bloemsma*, 1958.

Royal Dutch Touring Club A.N.W.B. office building and annexe, 5 Museumplein.
*H. Knijtijzer*, 1958.

Leidseplein Theatre, alterations to interior, Leidseplein. *A. N. Oyevaar and H. W. C. Stolle*, 1958.

Loos & Co.'s Fabriek N.V. Transformatorweg.
*Prof. H. T. Zwiers*, 1958.

Bus terminal, Marnixstraat.
*C. J. Henke*, 1958.

Renold Chains factory, Sloterdijk industrial area. *Arthur Staal*, 1959.

Dorr Oliver office building, Apollolaan. *Arthur Staal*, 1959.

Amsterdam Motel, Sloterweg on the main road from Amsterdam to The Hague. *Arthur Staal*, assisted by *A. J. Kleykamp*, 1959.

Netherlands Cancer Institute, extension of radiological department, 106 Sarphatistraat. *J. P. Kloos*. 1959,

A. H. Gerhard Home for the Aged, Slotermeerlaan. *W. van Tijen, M. Boom and Posno*, 1959.

Renault Garage, Mr. Treubplein. *W. S. van de Erve and R. van der Heyden*, 1959.

Gemeentelijk Administratiekantoor (Mutual Administration Office), Saïdjahstraat, Bos en Lommer. *B. Merkelbach and Prof. P. Elling*, 1959–1960.

Port of Amsterdam Authority office building, De Ruyterkade. *W. M. Dudok*, 1960.

Orphanage, Amstelveenseweg near IJsbaanpad. *Aldo van Eyck*, 1960.

"Vrije Universiteit" Protestant university buildings, Amstelveenseweg. *J. Groenewegen*, 1960.

'R.A.I.' exhibition hall, Europaplein. *A. Bodon*, 1960 onwards.

Railway post-office. *B. Merkelbach and Prof. P. Elling*, 1960 onwards.

Hospital, Jan van Galenstraat, Jan Tooropstraat, Jan Evertsenstraat. *Prof. F. P. J. Peutz*, 1960 onwards.

St Nicolas Grammar school, Prinses Irenestraat. *Lau Peters*, 1960.

Protestant church, 9 Van Ollefenstraat. *P. Zanstra*, 1960.

House, Apollolaan/Rubensstraat/Jan van Eyckstraat. *H. Salomonson*, 1960.

Office building, Trompkade. *F. J. E. Dekeukeleire*, 1960.

Apollo Hotel, near Apollolaan on the canal. *A. Bodon*, 1961–1962.

Hilton Hotel, August Allebéplein. *H. A. Maaskant, F. W. de Vlaming and H. Salm*, 1961.

Textile centre, Einsteinweg. *Maaskant, Van Dommelen, Kroes and Senf*, 1961 onwards.

House, Prinses Margrietstraat. *Onno Greiner*, 1960–1961.

Houses and workshops, 79–81 and 93–99 Rapenburgerstraat. *J. Brouwer and C. W. Schaling*, 1961.

Blocks of flats, Einsteinweg/L. van Vlaanderenstraat. *J. P. Kloos and Romke de Vries*, 1958–1961.

Nederlandsche Bank, Head Office, Frederiksplein. *Prof. M. F. Duintjer*, 1963 onwards.

Bus terminal, Musschenbroekstraat. *H. Vriend*, 1964.

APELDOORN

Home for the aged, Zwolseweg/Tennislaan. *Van Tijen, Boom and Posno*, 1959–1961.

Theatre, Loolaan. *B. Bijvoet and Prof. G. M. H. Holst*, 1965.

ARNHEM

Velperpoort railway station, Steenstraat. *K. van der Gaast*, 1953.

Railway station, Stationsplein. *H. G. J. Schelling*, 1954.

Gemeentelijk Energie- en Vervoerbedrijf (Municipal Power and Transport), Westervoortsedijk. *Prof. M. F. Duintjer*, 1949–1954.

Agfa office building, Boulevard, corner of Eusebiussingel. *C. Nap and G. J. P. van Ede*, 1959.

Bio Children's Holiday Centre, Wekeromseweg. *Dr. J. J. P. Oud*, 1959.

Block of flats and shops. Looyerstraat/Roggestraat/Velperplein. *H. Brouwer and T. T. Deurvorst*, 1959.

Municipal Administration office, Walburgstraat. *J. Konijnenburg*, 1960.

'Ciba' offices, Raapopseweg. *W. J. van Mourik and H. van Wely,* 1961.

Fine Arts Academy, Onderlangs.
*G. T. Rietveld,* 1961 – 1962.

## BENTVELD

House. *Jan Rietveld,* 1962.

## BERGEN (near Alkmaar)

Villa, 24 Eeuwige Laan. *J. J. Vriend,* 1953.

Villas, 35, 38, 41 Eeuwige Laan. *F. U. Verbruggen and P. R. Goldschmidt,* 1952, 1953 and 1955.

Villa, Parkweg. *A. Komter,* 1954.

Villa, Reigerslaan. *G. Boon,* 1955.

Villa, Buurweg. *J. Rietveld,* 1956.

Bungalow, 38 Eeuwige Laan.
*F. U. Verbruggen and P. R. Goldschmidt,* 1957.

Bungalow, Pier Panderweg.
*F. U. Verbruggen and P. R. Goldschmidt,* 1957.

Bungalow, 4 Wiertdijkje.
*F. U. Verbruggen and P. R. Goldschmidt,* 1957.

Block of flats, restaurant and bungalows, Van Wijckplein. *G. Boon,* 1958–1962.

Shopping centre, *Prof. J. H. van den Broek and Prof. J. B. Bakema,* 1960–1961.

## BERGEIJK

Textile factory, *G. T. Rietveld,* 1959.

Infant school, Lavendelstraat/Korenbloemstraat. *J. Strik,* 1959.

## BEVERWIJK

Factory of the Royal Netherlands Blast-Furnaces and Steelworks, Beyneslaan.
*B. Merkelbach and Prof. P. Elling,* 1949.

Railway station, Stationsplein.
*Prof. G. J. van der Grinten,* 1960.

## DE BILT

House, 33 Groenekanse Weg. *G. T. Rietveld,* 1958.

Juliana Flats, Julianalaan. *W. M. Dudok,* 1959.

## BILTHOVEN

Bungalow, Mozartlaan. *D. L. Steenberg, H. M. A. van Meer and G. van der Pol,* 1961.

## BREDA

Home for the aged, Flierstraat. *A. Evers and G. J. M. Sarlemijn.* 1950–1951.

Hispano Suiza factory, Terheydenseweg.
*Prof. J. H. van den Broek and Prof. J. B. Bakema,* 1951.

B.B.A. office building, Haagweg/Tramsingel.
*F. L. P. Dewald and G. van Setten,* 1958.

Boeimeer shopping centre. *E. F. Groosman,* 1958.

## BRIELLE

School adjoining the church. *Prof. J. H. van den Broek and Prof. J. B. Bakema,* 1950.

Horticultural school, Burgemeester van Sleenstraat. *Prof. J. H. van den Broek and Prof. J. B. Bakema,* 1956.

Primary school, Burgemeester van Sleenstraat.
*Prof. J. H. van den Broek and Prof. J. B. Bakema,* 1956.

Houses, Maarten Harpertszoon Trompstraat.
*Prof. J. H. van den Broek and Prof. J. B. Bakema,* 1956–1957.

Alterations to Town Hall. *Prof. J. H. van den Broek and Prof. J. B. Bakema,* 1957.

## BUSSUM

Block of flats, Nieuwe 's-Gravelandseweg.
*W. M. Dudok,* 1953–1954.

Church of the Redeemer, 59 H. A. Lorentzweg, corner of Ceintuurbaan. *Chr. Nielsen, J. H. C. Spruit and W. v. d. Kuilen,* 1956.

Block of flats adjoining shops and commercial bank, Veerstraat. *W. M. Dudok,* 1956–1957.

Flats, Vlietlaan, corner of Eslaan.
*K. v. d. Berg and E. J. Jurriens,* 1956.

‚De Gooise Warande' Home for the Aged, 19 Mezenlaan. *K. v. d. Berg and E. J. Jurriens*, 1958.

House, 53 Amersfoortsestraatweg.
*W. M. Dudok and R. M. H. Magnee*, 1958.

Town Hall, Brinklaan/Landstraat.
*Prof. C. Wegener Sleeswijk and S. J. S. Wichers*, 1958–1961.

## CUYK

Town Hall. *T. Taen and C. T. Nix*, 1958.

Infant school. *J. A. Elbers and A. J. M. Elbers*, 1957.

## DELFT

Houses, Tweemolentjeskade.
*W. van Tijen and H. A. Maaskant*, 1952.

Protestant home for the aged, Cort van der Lindenstraat. *A. Komter*, 1956–1960.

Heat and dust engineering laboratory (1953–1956), metallurgy laboratory (1954–1956), main metallurgy building (1958 onwards), aero- and hydrodynamics laboratory (1959 onwards), analytical chemistry laboratory (1959 onwards), reactor institute (1959 onwards), all for the Delft Institute of Advanced Technology, Wippolder. *Prof. J. H. van den Broek and Prof. J. B. Bakema*.

'Delfgauwse Weye' housing estate: houses, block of flats, home for the aged, infant school, community hall. *Prof. S. J. van Embden*, 1958–1959.

Immanuel Church (Protestant), Prof. Schoemakersstraat 1. *F. Eschauzier, A. van den Berg and P. de Vletter*, 1960.

Students' sport centre, Wippolder.
*Prof. P. Elling*, 1961.

Office building, van Miereveltlaan/W. van Helstlaan. *M. Reek and H. van Leeuwen* assisted by *H. Helle*, 1964.

## DELFZIJL

North Delfzijl residential area. *K. G. Olsmeyer*, 1957.

Advanced primary school. *J. J. M. Vegter*, 1959.

Algemene Bank Nederland, branch office, Marktstraat. *E. van Linge and A. van Linge*, 1959.

## DEN DOLDER

Villa, 11 Reelaan. *G. T. Rietveld*, 1950–1951.

Villa, 9 Tavernelaan. *G. T. Rietveld*, 1951–1952.

## DEN HELDER

Naval canteen, Kanaalweg. *Prof. C. Wegener Sleeswijk*, 1952–1954.

Church (Old-Catholic Church of Holland), Timorlaan. *Prof. H. T. Zwiers*, 1956.

Railway station. *Prof. G. J. van der Grinten*, 1958.

Municipal grammar school, Molukkenstraat. *Prof. Wieger Bruin*, 1958.

Secondary modern school, Timorlaan.
*Prof. Wieger Bruin*, 1955–1959.

## DEVENTER

Laboratory, Gooszenstraat. *J. W. C. Boks, W. Eijkelenboom and A. Middelhoek*, 1961.

## DIEMEN

Block of flats, Harteveldseweg.
*J. W. H. C. Pot and J. F. Pot-Keegstra*, 1951.

Gestetner N.V., 15 Muiderstraatweg.
*W. J. Kuiper and J. W. Kuiper*, 1956.

Diemeroord Institute.
*F. van Klingeren*, 1958.

## DIEREN

Crematorium and columbarium, Imboslaan. *H. C. P. Nuyten*, 1953.

## DORDRECHT

Office building, Stationsweg. *Maaskant, Van Dommelen, Kroos and Senf*, 1960.

Factory, Merwedestraat. *Maaskant,
Van Dommelen, Kroos and Senf,* 1961.

Grammar school, Baden Powelllaan/Noorden-
dijk. *F. J. Gouwetor and P. Mulder,* 1959–1962.

EERBEEK

Cultural centre, Jan Markesstraat.
*Han Schröder,* 1961–1962.

EINDHOVEN

Philips medical centre, Wilhelminaplein.
*Prof. H. T. Zwiers,* 1953.

Protestant church, Venstraat. *A. C. Nicolaï,*
1954.

Primary school, Laagstraat. *W. van Tijen,* 1954.

Railway station, goods shed.
*K. van der Gaast,* 1955–1956.

St Peter's Church. *L. R. T. Oskam,* 1956.

Church of the Resurrection (Protestant),
Alpenroosplein. *Prof. Wieger Bruin,* 1957.

Eindhoven Institute of Advanced Technology.
*Prof. S. J. van Embden,* 1957 onwards.

Roman Catholic primary school for girls,
Kardinaal de Jongweg. *A. J. N. Boosten,* 1959.

Town Hall. *J. A. van der Laan,* 1960 onwards.

Pharmacy and flats. *C. Valstar and
R. Tybout,* 1959.

Students' flats, Boutenslaan. *J. W. H. C. Pot
and J. F. Pot-Keegstra,* 1960.

Blocks of flats, Jacob van Maerlantlaan/
Boutenslaan/Busken Huetstraat/Willem Kloos-
laan. *J. Grijpma,* 1960.

Hotel and office building, Vestdijk.
*H. D. Bakker,* 1961.

Philips Nederland, Bosdijk.
*P. Verhare,* 1964.

Shop, Nieuwe Emmasingel.
*J. A. M. de Haan,* 1962–1963.

EMMELOORD

Post-office. *A. Komter,* 1952.

N.A.K. Offices (inspection service for
agricultural seeds), De Deel. *C. Nap and G. J. P.
van Ede,* 1957.

Agricultural Hall, De Deel.
*C. Nap and G. J. P. van Ede,* 1958.

Office building, De Deel. *Prof. S. J. van Embden,*
1960.

EMMEN

Grammar school, Oosterstraat.
*Y. S. Dijkstra,* 1947–1954.

Enkalon factory, 1st Bokslootweg.
*W. Masselink,* 1950–1952.

Houses. *Romke de Vries,* 1952–1956.

Herenhof Hotel, Wilhelminastraat.
*J. D. Nieman and S. F. Steeneken,* 1953.

Danlon factory, Bargermeer industrial site.
*Y. S. Dijkstra,* 1954–1955.

Open-Air Theatre, Markeweg. *Y. S. Dijkstra,*
1954.

Shops, Warmeerweg. *E. F. Groosman,* 1954.

Cinema, Oostingstraat. *A. C. Nicolaï,* 1954.

'De Nijkampen'. *A. C. Nicolaï,* 1955.

Houses, Emmermeer. *Romke de Vries,* 1953–
1958.

Villas, Meyerswegje. *Romke de Vries,*
1955–1958.

ENSCHEDE

Railway station, Stationsplein.
*H. G. J. Schelling,* 1952.

House, 150 Teesinklandenweg.
*H. Salomonson,* 1955–1956.

House, 133 Buursestraat.
*H. Salomonson,* 1956–1957.

Houses, Twekkelerveld. *J. W. H. C. Pot,
J. F. Pot-Keegstra and Prof. S. J. van Embden,*
1956–1957.

Municipal grammar school, 30 Lyceumlaan
*J. A. Kuiper,* 1957–1958.

Municipal Cleansing Dept. 1–1a Wethouder
Nijhuisstraat.
*H. Mastenbroek and J. H. de Herder*, 1956–1958.
Oliemolen Flats, Oliemolensingel.
*J. R. Koning and J. C. Rentjes*, 1958.
Hermes Flats, 1–9 The Boulevard, 31 Van
Loenshof, 55–58 H. J. van Heekplein.
*J. R. Koning and J. C. Rentjes*, 1957–1958.
Block of flats, houses and garages, Gronause-
straat. *F. Klein*, 1958.
Houses, Stadsveld. *J. Abma*, 1958–1959.
Protestant church, Wicher Nijkampstraat.
*P. Bügel*, 1958–1959.
Home for the aged, Gronausestraat.
*Prof. H. T. Zwiers*, 1959.
Enschede Institute of Advanced Technology.
*W. van Tijen, Prof. S. J. van Embden, P. Blom,
J. van Stigt and A. Nicolaï*, 1964 onwards.
Academy for Art and Industry, Roessinghs-
bleekweg/Maatmanweg. *A. Nicolaï* 1963–1964

## ETTEN-LEUR

'Tomado' factory. *H. A. Maaskant*, 1955.

## FLUSHING

Houses. *W. van Tijen and H. A. Maaskant*.
1947–1949.
Britannia Hotel, Evertsen Esplanade.
*J. W. C. Boks*, 1955–1960.

## GEERTRUIDENBERG

Power station. *J. A. G. van der Steur and
A. P. Wesselman van Helmond*, both of *J. van
Hasselt and De Koning's* office, 1953.
Elementary technical school.
*H. A. Maaskant and K. Bouman*, 1959.

## GELEEN

Church of the Cross. *Bart van Kasteel*, 1956.
'Hanenhof' Roman Catholic Youth Hostel.
*J. H. A. Huysmans*, 1957.

## GORINCHEM

Primary school. *Maaskant, Van Dommelen,
Kroos and Senf*, 1959.
Tall block of flats, Koningin Wilhelminastraat.
*Prof. S. J. van Embden*, 1960.

## GOUDA

St Michael's Primary School,
*J. J. Margry and Jacobs*, 1958.

## GRONINGEN

Block of flats, Ubbo Emmiussingel.
*F. Klein*, 1953.
Houses, Ubbo Emmiussingel. *K. G. Olsmeyer*,
1953.
Students' club, Grote Markt.
*J. J. M. Vegter*, 1953
'Arbeiderspers' N.V., publishers & printers, 25
Stoeldraaiersstraat. *J. J. M. Vegter*, 1954.
Furrier, 5–6 Grote Markt. *H. Salomonson and
J. H. Emck*, 1954.
'Galeries Modernes', department store, 27
Vismarkt. *F. Klein*, 1954.
Block of flats, Ossemarkt/Nieuwe Boteringe-
straat. *F. Klein*, 1954.
Bouman School, 6 Oldenbarneveltlaan.
*J. H. M. Wilhelm*, 1955.
Shops, houses, garage, 100–124 Oosterstraat.
*K. G. Olsmeyer*, 1955.
Villa, Kamplaan, *E. van Linge*, 1955.
Jan Evert Scholten School, Huygensstraat.
*J. H. M. Wilhelm*, 1956.
'Vihamij', office building, Antillenstraat.
*A. van Linge*, 1956.
Block of flats with shops, Linnaeusplein.
*P. Bügel*, 1956.
Offices, 7 Oosterhamrikkade.
*F. Klein and H. A. Maaskant*, 1956–1957.

'Kostverloren', block of houses, shops, central boiler-house, houses for the aged. *K. G. Olsmeyer*, 1956–1959.

Wester Flats. *K. G. Olsmeyer*, 1956.

Residential accommodation, College of Air Training, Eelde airfield. *Pierre Cuypers and F. P. Glastra van Loon*, 1957.

Minerva Flats, *K. G. Olsmeyer*, 1957.

Wielewaal Flats, Wielewaalplein and Zaagmuldersweg. *F. Klein*, 1957.

Offices, Zaagmuldersweg. *F. Klein*, 1957.

Mirte Church (Protestant), Linnaeusplein. *P. Bügel*, 1957.

Nurses' Home, Roman Catholic Hospital, Emmastraat. *Prof. G. H. M. Holt*, 1957.

Abbringh N.V., bookbinders, 12 Smirnoffstraat. *E. van Linge and A. van Linge*, 1958.

'Kwinke' Café-Restaurant, shops, houses and offices. *F. Klein*, 1958.

Shops and houses, Guldenstraat. *F. Klein*, 1958.

Alterations to shopping premises, 51 Herestraat. *Coen Bekink*, 1958.

Amsterdam-Rotterdam Bank N.V., Grote Markt. *J. J. M. Vegter*, 1958.

N.A.K. Offices (inspection service for agricultural seeds) 31 Vechtstraat. *P. Bügel*, 1958.

Groningse Industriële Crediet Bank N.V., Vechtstraat. *E. van Linge and A. van Linge*, 1959.

Technical school, Antillenstraat. *J. J. M. Vegter*, 1959.

Business premises of Northern Readers' Club, Vechtstraat, *P. Bügel*, 1959.

Roman Catholic Church, Landsteinerlaan/Koekstraat. *C. H. Bekink*, 1959.

Municipal building for several departments, social and medical care, Radesingel/Trompstraat. *Bureau Van Linge*, 1961–1963.

Home for the aged, Kochstraat/Galenusstraat. *van Tijen, Boom and Posno, and M. D. van Wensveen*, 1961–1963.

Home for the aged, Boerhaavelaan. *Coen Bekink*, 1960–1963.

## HAARLEM

Mendel College, Orionweg, North Haarlem, *Prof. G. H. M. Holt*, 1955.

House, 35 Middenlaan, *Prof. G. H. M. Holt*, 1956.

Merck, Sharp & Dohme, pharmaceutical factory, Nijverheidsweg. *Prof. J. F. Berghoef and H. Klarenbeek*, 1958.

Merck, Sharp & Dohme, extension of stores and offices, Nijverheidsweg. *H. A. Maaskant*, 1959.

Nederland-Kattenburg Co. N.V. clothing store, 36 Grote Houtstraat. *H. A. Maaskant*, 1958.

'Gillis' houses, Schoolmeesterlaan, Jan Bontelaan, Jan de Mijterlaan. Pieter Wanklaan. *H. W. Brakel and W. Buma*, 1958.

Houses, Haspelstraat. *H. W. Brakel and W. Buma*, 1958.

Tuberculosis Clinic, Consultation Bureau, 77 Orionweg. *Prof. H. T. Zwiers*, 1958.

Roman Catholic church and presbytery, Prins Bernhardlaan. *Prof. G. H. M. Holt*, 1958.

Delftwijk shopping centre. *E. F. Groosman* assisted by *T. Brouwer*, 1959.

Offices and business premises, 55 and 57 Spaarne. *F. J. E. Dekeukeleire*, 1957 and 1959.

Roman Catholic church, Prinses Beatrixlaan/Kromhoutlaan. *Prof. G. H. M. Holt*, 1961.

## THE HAGUE

Railway post-office, *G. C. Bremer*, 1948.

Van der Heem, Factory recreation building, 256 Maanweg. *W. S. van de Erve*, 1952.

Shopping centre, Heeswijkplein.
*F. Ottenhof,* 1953.

House, Ereprijsweg. *Romke de Vries,* 1953–1954.

Flats, Sportlaan. *P. Zanstra,* 1954.

Grotius Grammar School, Klaverstraat.
*S. Schamhart,* 1954.

Primary schools, Steenwijklaan.
*H. A. Maaskant,* 1954.

Home for the aged, Goetlijfstraat.
*Prof. H. T. Zwiers,* 1954.

'De Nederlanden van 1845', office building, partially built in 1926 by Berlage and completed in 1954 by *W. M. Dudok* in accordance with Berlage's plans. 2 Groenhovenstraat.

St. Paul's Church (Protestant), 35a Sijzenlaan.
*Prof. J. F. Berghoef and H. Klarenbeek,* 1954.

Shopping centre, Westhovenplein.
*H. C. P. Nuyten,* 1955.

Home for the aged, 120 Twickelstraat.
*F. Ottenhof,* 1955.

Zorgvliet Church (Protestant), 5–7 Jan Willem Frisolaan. *C. Westerduin and M. Kuyper,* 1955.

House built on a bunker, Ruychrocklaan.
*Romke de Vries,* 1955.

Protestant church, Hengelolaan. *K. L. Sijmons,* 1955.

Maisonettes, Meppelweg. *F. Ottenhof,* 1956.

Grammar School,
Goudsbloemlaan/Segbroeklaan.
*Dr. J. J. P. Oud,* 1953.

'Nutsspaarbank' (savings bank) branch office, Almeloplein. *J. A. Lucas and H. E. Niemeyer,* 1956.

'Nutsspaarbank' (savings bank) branch office, Theresiastraat. *J. A. Lucas and H. E. Niemeyer,* 1956.

Houses, Corn. Houtmanstraat.
*J. J. M. Vegter and H. Brouwer,* 1956.

Wilhelmina Church (Protestant), 6 Louise Henriëttestraat. *Prof. H. T. Zwiers,* 1956.

Rudolf Blik N.V., electrical appliances and hardware factory, Laakkanaal.
*W. S. van de Erve,* 1957.

Succes N.V. office-building, Celebesstraat.
*W. S. van de Erve,* 1957.

Morgenstond (II) District, blocks bounded by Steenwijklaan, Enschedelaan, Coevordenstraat and Zwartsluisstraat. *Romke de Vries,* 1956–1959.

Caltex offices, Verhulstplein.
*Prof. C. Wegener Sleeswijk and S. J. S. Wichers,* 1957.

Protestant church, Medlerstraat/Heeswijkplein.
*Prof. C. Wegener Sleeswijk and S. J. S. Wichers,* 1957.

Block of flats, Goudsbloemlaan. *J. B. van Bruggen, G. Drexhage and J. J. Sterkenburg,* 1958.

Zuiderpark Secondary School, Zuidlarenstraat.
*S. Schamhart,* 1958.

Montessori Grammar School, 5 Nassau Bredastraat. *J. J. Hornstra and Boudewijns,* 1958.

Roman Catholic Church of St. Anthony and St. Louis, 326 Leyweg ('Morgenstond').
*W. Wouters and Prof. F. P. J. Peutz,* 1958.

School, Exlostraat. *J. A. Lucas and H. E. Niemeyer,* 1958.

Two blocks of bachelor flats, Hart Nibbrigkade, corner of Breitnerlaan. *D. Zuiderhoek,* 1959.

Elizabeth Arden establishment, 24 Plaats.
*Romke de Vries,* 1957–1959.

Housing estate with shopping centre, Beresteinplein (part of Berestein project, end of Meppelweg near Lozerlaan). *Romke de Vries,* 1957–1959.

American Embassy, Tournooiveld, opposite the Royal Theatre. *Marcel Breuer,* 1959.

Local telephone exchange, Taco Scheltemastraat. *H. A. Maaskant,* 1959.

Headquarters of the Postal Giro Services, Adelheidstraat. *Prof. J. H. van den Broek and Prof. J. B. Bakema*, 1959.

'Nederlanden van 1845' office building, Verhulstplein. *Prof. C. Wegener Sleeswijk and S. J. S. Wichers*, 1959.

Tall blocks of flats, Meer en Bos-Kijkduin, Heliotrooplaan. *W. S. van de Erve*, 1959.

Tall blocks of flats, West Vrederust, *C. Pet*, 1959 onwards.

Department of Scientific and Industrial Research Headquarters. *P. Zanstra*, 1959 onwards.

'Nillmij' office building, Houtrustbrug. *H. Brouwer and T. T. Deurvorst*, 1960.

Congress building, Johan de Wittlaan. *Dr. J. J. P. Oud*, 1960 onwards.

Block of flats for single women, De Savornin Lohmanplein. *J. W. H. C. Pot, J. F. Pot-Keegstra and G. Westerhout*, 1959.

Protestant church, 143 Laan van Nieuw Oost-Indië. *G. Drexhage*, 1960.

Villa, St. Hubertusweg. *H. van Leeuwen*, 1960.
Villa, Ruychrocklaan/Van Soutelandelaan. *G. T. Rietveld*, 1960.

Pier, Scheveningen. *Apon, Dijk and Maaskant*, 1960.

Extension Municipal Museum (Berlage), Stadhouderslaan. *S. Schamhart and J. F. Heijligers*, 1960.

'Nezam' offices, Johan de Wittlaan/Jan Willem Frisolaan. *A. W. P. Thunnissen*, 1960–1961.

Kamer van Koophandel en Fabrieken van 's-Gravenhage (The Hague Chamber of Commerce) Alexander Gogelweg.
*Jan Wils and M. J. B. Meijer*, 1962–1963.

K.L.M. air terminal and offices, Grote Marktstraat. *Prof. J. H. van den Broek and Prof. J. B. Bakema*, 1963.

Fish Auction Hall, Scheveningen harbour, *Sj. Schamhart e.a.*

Staatsdrukkerij (Government printing office), Boomsluiterskade/Christ. Plantijnstraat. *W. S. van Erve* 1964–1965.

## HARDEGARIJP
House and office, *A. Bonnema*, 1961

## HAREN
Home for the aged, Middelhorstweg. *A. C. Nicolaï*, 1952–1953.
Groningen School, Appelbergen, near Glimmen. *J. H. M. Wilhelm*, 1954.
Church of St. Nicolas, Beatrixlaan/Irenelaan. *J. Dresmé*, 1962.

## HAZERSWOUDE
Town Hall, Rijndijk. *Maaskant, Van Dommelen, Kroos and Senf.* 1962–1963.

## HEERJANSDAM
Town Hall. *Leo de Jonge and M. L. Dorst*, 1959.
Villa, *E. Kramer*, 1959–1960.

## HEERLEN
Town Hall, Raadhuisplein. *Prof. F. P. J. Peutz*, 1939–1947.
Vroom & Dreesmann, department store, Klompstraat. *Prof F. P. J. Peutz*, 1946.
Gas and Electricity Company, partially built, Gringel. *Prof. F. P. J. Peutz*, 1948.
Teachers' training college, Schondelermolenweg. *Prof. F. P. J. Peutz*, 1953.
Roman Catholic Church of St Anne, Bakkerveld, *Prof. F. P. J. Peutz*, 1953.
L.T.M. office building, Kempensweg/Kloosterweg. *Prof. F. P. J. Peutz*, 1957.
Meulenberg business premises, Akerstraat/Putgroef. *Prof. F. P. J. Peutz*, 1957.
Hospital extension, Putgraaf. *Prof. F. P. J. Peutz*, 1957–1958.

Nurses' Home, 'Aan het groene boord'.
*Prof. F. P. J. Peutz*, 1957–1958.

Limagas building, Schaesbergerweg.
*Prof. F. P. J. Peutz*, 1958.

Vroom & Dreesmann, department store.
*Prof. F. P. J. Peutz*, 1958.

Theatre, Het Loon. *B. Bijvoet and Prof. F. P. J. Peutz*, 1959.

Rivoli Cinema, Parallelweg. *Prof. F. P. J. Peutz*, 1959.

Vegers Furniture Store, Spoorsingel/Willem-straat. *Wolfs and Seelen*, 1959.

Home for the aged, Aarveld.
*Prof. G. H. M. Holt*, 1959.

Office building, Schinkelstraat.
*G. J. W. Snelder*, 1960.

## HENDRIK-IDO-AMBACHT

Holland N.V. offices. *P. H. Cuyperus*, 1958.

## HENGELO

Primary school, Prins Bernhardplantsoen.
*D. J. Schenk*, 1950.

Railway station, Stationsplein.
*H. G. J. Schelling*, 1951.

'De Telgen', shop and office building, Markt.
*G. Feenstra and E. H. van Broekhuizen*, 1958.

Town Hall, *Prof. J. F. Berghoef and H. Klaren-beek*, 1959 onwards.

'Klein Driene', houses, Mozartlaan.
*Prof. J. H. van den Broek and Prof. J. B. Bakema*, 1958–1959.

## 's-HERTOGENBOSCH

Stadium, Rijksweg Oost.
*Prof. G. H. M. Holt*, 1952.

Shopping centre, Chr. Huygensweg and Copernicuslaan. *Prof. G. H. M. Holt*, 1955.

Nicholson File factory, Rietveldenweg.
*H. A. Maaskant and K. Bouman*, 1957.

Verenigde Schoenmachinefabriek (United Shoe Machine factory), Branderijstraat.
*H. A. Maaskant and K. Bouman*, 1957.

'De Kruithoorn', powder mill.
*H. A. Maaskant*, 1958.

Walloon Church, Zuiderparkweg.
*H. Knijtijzer*, 1958.

Police station. *Prof. M. F. Duintjer*, 1959–1960.

Western Plan group of schools.
*Prof. H. T. Zwiers*, 1959.

Office building, Smalle Haven.
*H. M. van de Vrede and L. C. van der Lee*, 1960.

Block of flats with external access galleries, Palestrinastraat. *B. Hooykaas and B. van Veen*, 1960–1962.

Provincial Administration Building, *Maaskant, Van Dommelen, Kroos and Senf*, 1964 onwards.

## HILVERSUM

Villa, 98 Noodweg, *B. Bijvoet and Prof. G. H. M. Holt*, 1951.

Villa, Blesboklaan. *A. Bodon*, 1953.

Block of flats, Jacob van Campenlaan.
*W. M. Dudok*, 1954.

Eastern station, Over 't Spoor.
*K. van der Gaast*, 1954.

Protestant primary school, Lieven de Keylaan.
*F. Eschauzier, F. van den Berg and P. de Vletter*, 1956.

'Corverbos', block of flats for single women, Schitterweg. *Jan Dullaart*, 1956.

Block of flats, 's-Gravelandseweg, corner of Bussumerweg. *W. M. Dudok*, 1957.

Da Costa School, Lieven de Keylaan.
*Paul de Vletter*, 1957.

Verenigde Gooise Melkbedrijven (United Dairies), 34 Larenseweg. *H. M. Martens and A. J. Kramer*, 1957.

132

Grammar school, 35 Witte Kruislaan.
*Pierre Cuypers*, 1957.
Studio unit for Radio Nederland International Service, Lage Naarderweg/Nieuwe Craailoseweg. *Prof. J. H. van den Broek and Prof. J. B. Bakema*, 1958–1960.
Printing works and office building, 4 Zeverijnstraat. *W. M. Dudok and R. M. H. Magnee*, 1958.
VARA broadcasting studio extension, Heuvellaan. *B. Merkelbach and Prof. P. Elling*, 1959.
Elementary technical school, Pieter Postlaan. *Paul de Vletter*, 1960.
Nurses' Home, Nassaulaan/Rembrandtlaan. *W. G. Elshuis*, 1961.
Bethlehem Church (Protestant), Diependaalse Laan/Loosdrechtseweg. *D. Zuiderhoek*, 1963.

## HUIZEN

Villa, Sterrenboslaan. *J. Rietveld*, 1956.
Villa, Nieuwe Blaricumerweg. *D. L. Sterenberg, H. M. A. van Meer and G. van der Pol*, 1957–1958.

## ILPENDAM

Villa, Monnickendammer Rijweg.
*G. T. Rietveld*, 1958.

## KATWIJK

Houses, Molenblok. *B. Merkelbach and Prof. P. Elling*, 1953–1954.
Noordzee Hotel, shops, etc.
Esplanade, corner of Voorstraat.
*C. Drexhage*, 1953.
Houses, Rijnmond. *Prof. S. J. van Embden*, 1957.

## KINDERDIJK

Villa, Puntweg. *G. T. Rietveld*, 1948–1949.

## LEEUWARDEN

Protestant Church, Troelstraplein.
*A. C. Nicolaï*, 1954.
t' Heechtterp', houses, Archipelweg.
*Prof. J. H. van den Broek and Prof. J. B. Bakema*, 1958 onwards.

## LEIDEN

Houses, Da Costastraat, along Leiden-Woerden railway line, and Boshuizerkade. *J. A. Kuiper, F. J. Gouwetor, J. de Ranitz and R. D. Bleeker*, 1952–1953.
Railway station, Stationsplein.
*H. G. J. Schelling*, 1953.
Bus terminal.
*H. G. J. Schelling*, 1956.
Block of flats, Kanaalweg. *E. F. Groosman*, 1958.
Students' flats, Churchilllaan. *H. Postel*, 1959.
'Boerhaave' University quarter, Mariënpoelstraat/Boerhaavelaan. *E. F. Groosman*, 1960.
Student's club "Minerva", Breestraat.
*J. W. C. Boks, W. Eijkelboom and A. Middelhoek*, 1965.

## LEIDERDORP

Home for the aged, Mauritssingel.
*Jan Heese*, 1963–1964.

## LEIDSCHENDAM

Postal and Telecommunications Services laboratory (Neher Laboratory). *Prof. S. J. van Embden*, 1956.

## LOCHEM

Police station, Prins Bernhardweg.
*G. K. Veeze and F. J. Twijnstra*, 1959.

## MAASTRICHT

Houses, Koningsplein.
*F. C. J. Dingemans, 1950–1951.*
Block of flats, Fatimaplein.
*F. C. J. Dingemans, 1955.*
Home for the aged, Servaesbolwerk.
*J. H. A. Huysmans, 1955.*
Primary school, Hunnenweg/Regentlaan.
*A. J. N. Boosten, 1956.*
Primary school, Frans van Laarstraat/Ravelijnstraat. *A. H. J. Swinkels and B. H. F. L. Salemans, 1957.*
Block of flats, Oranjeplein.
*A. J. N. Boosten, 1958.*
Shops and houses, Clavecimbelstraat.
*G. J. W. Snelder, 1959.*
Tall block of flats, Oranjeplein.
*Prof. G. H. M. Holt, 1960.*
Advanced Primary School, Kolonel Ritterstraat. *A. J. N. Boosten, 1959.*
Villa, Scharnerweg, *G. J. W. Snelder, 1960.*
Tuberculosis Clinic, Becanusstraat.
*G. J. W. Snelder, 1961.*
Church ofa St. Ann, Dr. van Kleefstraat.
*T. H. A. Boosten, 1964.*

## MEPPEL

Houses for the aged, Woldkade.
*Romke de Vries, 1949–1950.*
Protestant church, Herengracht.
*H. Knijtijzer, 1951.*
School buildings, teachers' training college, seven-class primary school, infant school, Goeman Borgesiusweg. *H. A. Maaskant, 1957.*

## MIDDELBURG

Central Training School for Military Administration, Noordstraat. *E. F. Groosman, 1949.*

Griffioen (Griffin) Park. *A. Rothuizen and P. J. 't Hooft, 1954.*

## MIJDRECHT

Johnson's Wax Int. Ltd., offices and factory.
*H. A. Maaskant, 1964 onwards.*

## NAGELE

Houses, schools, shopping centre, church, etc., designed by *Prof. J. H. van den Broek and Prof. J. B. Bakema, Romke de Vries, Aldo van Eyck, J. Rietveld. J. Niegeman, W. van Bodegraven, Lotte Stam and E. F. Groosman, 1955 onwards.*

## NOORDWIJK

Experimental radar laboratory, Koningin Astridboulevard. *Oyevaar, Stolle and Van Gool, 1959–1960.*
Villa, Ligusterweg. *G. T. Rietveld, 1960.*
Youth hostel, Langevelderlaan.
*F. van Klingeren, 1960.*
De Baak Hotel, Koningin Astridboulevard.
*A. C. Gathier, 1961.*

## NIMEGUEN

'Heseveld' group of houses, Dennenstraat, Jacob van Campenstraat, Molenweg.
*A. Evers and G. J. M. Sarlemijn, 1952–1953.*
Nederlandsche Bank. *Prof. H. T. Zwiers, 1954.*
Block of flats, Trianusplein, corner of Mr. Franckenstraat. *H. Nefkens, 1955.*
Houses, flats and offices, corner of Stikke Hezelstraat/Augustijnenstraat. *Prof. H. Brouwer and F. W. de Vlaming, 1956.*
Houses and shops, corner of Stikke Hezelstraat/Houtstraat. *H. van Vreeswijk, 1955.*
Gelderland paper factory, Industriehaven.
*J. A. G. van der Steur, A. P. Wesselman van Helmond and H. C. Stadlander, 1958.*

Roman Catholic advanced primary school, Archipelstraat. *Prof. G. H. M. Holt*, 1958.

"Star Flats", 81–175 Heidebloemstraat. *A. van der Kloot*, 1958.

"Star Flats", 2–136 Batavierenweg. *H. Nefkens*, 1958.

Friden Holland factory, 15 Tennismolenweg. *F. W. de Vlaming and H. Salm*, 1958.

Hema, department store, 5 Grote Markt. *A. Elzas*, 1958.

Hatertse Veld residential area. *E. F. Groosman* assisted by *P. C. Bos*, 1959.

University buildings (mathematics and physics), Driehuizerweg. *Prof. F. P. J. Peutz*, 1959 onwards.

Hotel, Keizer Karelplein. *J. W. C. Boks*, 1960 onwards.

Theatre, Keizer Karelplein. *B. Bijvoet and Prof. G. H. M. Holt*, 1960 onwards.

Factory and office, Graafse weg. *F. W. de Vlaming and H. Salm*, 1960.

Chapel, St. Augustinus Monastery, 274 Graafse weg. *Prof. G. J. van der Grinten*, 1963.

## OEGSTGEEST

Montessori School, Louise de Colignylaan. *J. P. Kloos*, 1954.

House, 56 Hofbrouckerlaan. *G. J. van der Grinten*, 1959.

## OOSTELIJK FLEVOLAND (East Flevoland)

Colijn pumping station. *Roosenburg, P. Verhave and J. G. E. Luyt*, 1955.

Lovink pumping station. *Roosenburg, P. Verhave and J. G. E. Luyt*, 1955.

Wortman pumping station. *Roosenburg, P. Verhave and J. G. E. Luyt*, 1955.

## OOSTERBEEK

Blocks of flats in the Bato district. *J. Grijpma*, 1953–1954.

'Sonnenberg', Home for Retired Teachers 13 v. Borsselenweg. *J. Grijpma*, 1957.

Paasberg Flats, Overzicht. *G. Bruins*, 1958.

Villa, Beelaertslaan. *J. Verhoeven*, 1959–1960.

## OSS

Organon's Cortison N.V., building. *A. P. Wesselman van Helmond and J. A. G. van der Steur*, 1956.

Synagogue, Smalstraat/Oude Kerkstraat. *Jos Bijnen*, 1959.

## OTTERLO

Pavilion for plastic art exhibitions, National Park „de Hoge Veluwe", originally built in Sonsbeek Park, Arnhem. *G. T. Rietveld*, 1954–1955.

## OUDESCHOOT

Factories, Wolff and Zimmer, *Portland, Ore.*, U.S.A. and *J. Abma*, 1962.

## PAPENDRECHT

Shopping centre. *J. den Hartog*, 1963.

## PURMEREND

Railway station. *K. F. G. Spruit*, 1958.

## REEUWIJK

Villa. *H. Salomonson*, 1963.

## ROTTERDAM

Industrial flats, Oostzeedijk. *W. van Tijen and H. A. Maaskant*, 1947.

Industrial flats, Goudsesingel.
*W. van Tijen and H. A. Maaskant*, 1947–1949.

Van Melle biscuit and toffee factories, Olympiaweg. *A. Bodon and Cysouw*, 1948.

't Venster (The Window) Cinema.
*Prof. J. H. van den Broek and Prof. J. B. Bakema*, 1948.

Groothandelsgebouw (Wholesale trade building, 45 Stationsplein.
*W. van Tijen and H. A. Maaskant*, 1948–1951.

'Bouwcentrum', International Building and Housing Information Centre, Weena.
*J. W. C. Boks*, 1948 and 1955.

H.A.L. embarkation and disembarkation hall, warehouse and work-shop, Wilhelminakade, Rijnhaven. *J. A. Brinkman and Prof. J. H. van den Broek*, 1937–1953.

Bonders, Rijnhaven. *M. Lockhorst and W. Overeynder*, 1949.

Handelsveem (storage company), Rijnhaven. *De Ruyter and van der Graaf*, 1949.

Blaauwhoedenveem (storage company), Rijnhaven. *P. Kanters*, 1949.

Residential building, Zuidplein.
*W. van Tijen and H. A. Maaskant*, 1949.

Houses, Vredenoordlaan. *Prof. J. H. van den Broek and Prof. J. B. Bakema*, 1949.

Spaanse Polder industrial buildings.
*W. van Tijen and H. A. Maaskant*, 1950–1952.

'Ahoy' and 'E. 55' exhibition halls, Wijtemaweg. *Prof. J. H. van den Broek and Prof. J. B. Bakema*, 1950 and 1955.

House, Hillegersberg. *H. Haan*, 1951.

Municipal transport and motor service, cleansing department, Blijdorpplein. *J. A. Brinkman, Prof. J. H. van den Broek and Prof. J. B. Bakema*, 1951–1954.

Ter Meulen, Wassen and Van Vorst, shops, 3–31 Binnenweg. *Prof. J. H. van den Broek and Prof. J. B. Bakema*, 1951.

Business premises and house, Wijnstraat.
*W. Vermeer*, 1951–1952.

Nederland-Kattenburg, clothing store, 8 Beursplein. *W. van Tijen and H. A. Maaskant*, 1952.

Baptist church, 1–3 Noordmolenwerf.
*G. T. J. Kuiper*, 1951.

W. van Houten & Zn., (metal company), 9 Bierstraat. *Prof. J. H. van den Broek and Prof. J. B. Bakema*, 1952.

Professor J. H. van den Broek's house, 45 Kralingseweg. *Prof. J. H. van den Broek and Prof. J. B. Bakema*, 1952.

Grain warehouse of the marketing organization of the Netherlands Co-operative Societies, Veerlaan. *J. J. M. Vegter*, 1952.

Houses in 'Zuidwijk'. *W. van Tijen and H. A. Maaskant, Romke de Vries and E. F. Groosman, W. van Tijen, M. Boom and Posno, Jos and Leo de Jonge, A. Krijgsman, Vermeer and Van Herwaarden, etc.*, 1952 onwards.

Van Stolk's Office building, 26 Delftse Vaart. *W. van Tijen and H. A. Maaskant*, 1952.

Peek en Cloppenburg, clothing store, 200 Hoogstraat. *E. H. and H. M. Kraayvanger*.

Vaerhorst shopping centre, Zuidwijk.
*E. F. Groosman*, 1952.

Lijnbaan shopping centre. *Prof. J. H. van den Broek and Prof. J. B. Bakema*, 1953.

H.H. de Klerk, furniture store, 7 Binnenweg.
*Prof. J. H. van den Broek and Prof. J. B. Bakema*, 1953.

Jungerhans, stores, 3–5 Binnenweg. *E. H. and H. M. Kraayvanger*, 1953.

Houses, Willemsplein.
*E. H. and H. M. Kraayvanger*, 1953.

Dockworkers' Labour Exchange, Bananenstraat. *Prof. J. H. van den Broek and Prof. J. B. Bakema*, 1953.

Synagogue, Bentincklaan.
*J. van Duyn and Baars*, 1954.

Rotterdams Nieuwsblad (newspaper), Coolsingel/Binnenweg. *Prof. F. A. Eschauzier*, 1954.

'Arbeiderspers', publishers and printers, Slaak.
*J. J. M. Vegter*, 1954.

Gerrit de Koker Home for the Aged, Gerdesiaweg. *H. D. Bakker*, 1954.

Anton Huf Jr. shoe store, 183 Hoogstraat.
*Prof. J. H. van den Broek and Prof. J. B. Bakema*, 1954.

Maastoren flats. *H. D. Bakker*, 1955.

Auction hall for semi-tropical fruits, 25 Marconistraat. *W. van Tijen and H. A. Maaskant*, 1955.

Lumière Cinema, Kruiskade, corner of Lijnbaan. *A. Bodon*, 1955.

Houses and shops, Hoogstraat.
*B. Merkelbach and Prof. P. Elling*, 1955.

Groenendaal Flats.
*W. van Tijen and H. A. Maaskant*, 1955.

Doctors' houses, Zuidplein-Goereesestraat.
*Prof. J. H. van den Broek and Prof. J. B. Bakema*, 1955.

Houses in Pendrecht. *J. A. Lucas and H. F. Niemeyer, H. D. Bakker, Jos and Leo de Jonge, E. F. Groosman, H. Nefkens, J. A. Kuiper, F. J. Gouwetor and J. de Ranitz, J. W. C. Boks*, etc., 1955 onward.

Protestant church, Zuidwijk.
*H. W. M. Hupkes and W. C. van Asperen*, 1955.

Shell Netherlands refinery, chemical plants and central office at Pernis, Vondelingenweg.
*C. A. Abspoel*, 1956.

Gilda toffee and caramel factory, Schuttevaerweg, Spaanse Polder. *H. A. Maaskant and K. Bouman*, 1956.

Galeries Modernes, department store, Hoogstraat. *Prof. J. H. van den Broek and Prof. J. B. Bakema*, 1956.

'De Nieuwe Markt' shopping centre.
*H. D. Bakker*, 1956.

Maria Moll Foundation houses for single women, Van Beethovensingel. *J. W. C. Boks*, 1957.

Block of flats, shops and café, 13 storeys, Aert van Nesstraat. *H. D. Bakker*, 1957.

Block of flats, café and garages, Van Ghentstraat, 9 storeys. *H. D. Bakker*, 1957.

Block of flats with garages and one floor consisting of doctors' consulting rooms.
*A. Krijgsman*, 1957.

St. Lucia Roman Catholic Training School for Girls, Hennekijnstraat. *Leo de Jonge*, 1957.

Shops and flats, 3 storeys, Karel Doormanstraat.
*A. Krijgsman*, 1957.

Flats, shops, offices and garages, 14 storeys, Kruiskade. *H. A. Maaskant*, 1957.

Flats, shops and garages, 9 storeys, Van Ghentstraat. *H. A. Maaskant*, 1957.

Shops and flats, 3 storeys, Karel Doormanstraat.
*H. A. Maaskant*, 1957.

Showroom, office, central hall, 33 Delftsestraat.
*H. A. Maaskant*, 1957.

Savings bank, Botersloot. *Dr. J. J. P. Oud*, 1957.

De Bijenkorf department store, Coolsingel.
*Marcel Breuer and A. Elzas*, 1957.

Office building, 14 storeys, Schiedamsedijk/Schildersstraat. *H. D. Bakker*, 1958.

'Trouw' newspaper offices, Witte de Withstraat. *C. Elffers*, 1958.

'Columeta' office building, 50 Eendrachtsweg,
*Rein H. Fledderus* 1958.

Block of flats, Westzeedijk, corner of Kievitslaan. *E. F. Groosman* assisted by *P. C. Bos*, 1958.

137

Shipyard canteen, Waalhaven.
*E. F. Groosman*, 1958.

'Asterlo', group of houses, Zuidwijk.
*E. F. Groosman*, 1958.

Rijn Hotel, youth hostel and youth centre, annex, Mauritsweg, corner of Schouwburgplein. *B. Merkelbach and Prof. P. Elling*, 1959.

Montessori Grammar School. Schimmelpenninckstraat, *Prof. J. H. van den Broek and Prof. J. B. Bakema*, 1959.

"Utrecht" Insurance Co., Coolsingel opposite Town Hall. *Dr. J. J. P. Oud*, 1959.

'Nieuwe Matex' office building, Rotterdam Botlek, Welplaatweg, Spijkenisse. *J. W. C. Boks, W. Eykelenboom and A. Middelhoek*, 1959.

'V.O.S.' and 'M.A.B.I.' office building, combined office building for inland water transport and towage. *J. W. C. Boks, W. Eykelenboom and A. Middelhoek*, 1959.

Protestant church of St. Paul, Mauritsweg. *B. Hooykaas, B. van Veen and A. de Jong*, 1959.

Block of flats, Kralingseweg. *H. D. Bakker*, 1959.

'Eerste Nederlandse Verz. Mij.' (First Netherlands Insurance Company), offices, restaurant and cabaret-dance hall, Coolsingel. *J. P. van Bruggen, C. Drexhage, J. J. Sterkenburg and A. Bodon*, 1959.

Shops, offices, Westblaak/Hartmanstraat. *E. H. Kraayvanger and H. M. Kraayvanger*, 1959.

Railway post-office, Delftseplein. *E. H. Kraayvanger and H. M. Kraayvanger*, 1960.

Showrooms, industrial buildings, Zuidplein. *H. A. Maaskant*, 1960.

Dijkzigt Hospital. *Municipal Office of Public Works*, 1960.

Waalhaven Power Station. *Municipal Office of Public Works*, 1960.

Shell Tankers N.V., office building and filling station, Schiekade. *C. A. Abspoel*, 1960.

Municipal Grammar School, Argonautenweg. *J. A. Kuiper, F. J. Gouwetor and J. de Ranitz*, 1960 onwards.

Office building, Stadhuisplein. *Prof. J. H. van den Broek, Prof. J. B. Bakema, J. M. A. de Groot*, 1960 onwards.

Concert Hall. *Rein H. Fledderus, E. H. and H. M. Kraayvanger*, 1960 onwards.

Catholic church, Slinge. *Harry Nefkens*, 1960.

Office building, Terwenakker/Maasboulevard. *J. W. C. Boks, W. Eykelenboom and A. Middelhoek*, 1960.

Euromast restaurant. *H. A. Maaskant and Municipal Office of Public Works*, 1960.

Carbon factory, Botlekweg. *J. Verster*, 1959–1960.

'De Hoofdpoort' office building, Westblaak. *E. H. and H. M. Kraayvanger and C. F. A. Knol*, 1960–1962.

Office building, Westzeedijk/Zalmhaven. *P. K. A. Pennink*, 1962.

Office building, Marconiplein. *F. U. Verbruggen and P. R. Goldschmidt*, 1964 onwards.

RIJSWIJK

Blocks of flats, Hoorn Bridge. *J. A. Lucas and H. E. Niemeyer*, 1955.

Houses built on the 'Iboco' system, Karel Doormanlaan. *Prof. J. H. van den Broek and Prof. J. B. Bakema*, 1955.

Motel, Jan Thijssenweg. *W. Verschoor and W. H. Verschoor*, 1956.

'Onderwatershof', Home for the Aged.
*J. J. Hornstra and J. Gerbracht, 1957.*

Duiker Apparatenfabriek N.V. Factory, Plaspoel Polder. *H. A. Maaskant, 1959.*

Protestant church, Generaal Berenschotlaan. *Leo de Jonge* assisted by *M. L. Dorst, 1959.*

Office building, Hendrik Ravesteijnplein. *J. A. Lucas and H. E. Niemeyer, 1960.*

Laboratory, Bataafse Internationale Petroleum Maatschappij, Lange Kleiweg/Volmerlaan. *M. F. D. Division, architecture section, 1959–1961.*

Protestant church, Dr. Colijnlaan. *Prof. M. F. Duintjer, 1962.*

'In den Boogaard' shopping centre. *J. A. Lucas and H. E. Niemeyer, 1963 onwards.*

## SANTPOORT

Villa, Harddraverslaan. *G. Th. Rietveld, 1960.*

Protestant church, Willem de Zwijgerlaan/Duinweg. *J. Kruger, 1960.*

## SCHIEDAM

Houses, Troelstralaan/Van Haarenlaan. *E. F. Groosman, 1952–1954.*

House, Julianalaan. *Romke de Vries, 1953–1954.*

Manometer factory, Nieuwepoortweg. *F. Swaneveld and S. Th. Goslinga, 1955.*

Block of flats, Rotterdamse Dijk. *W. H. Spruyt and G. den Butter, 1955.*

Reformed church, Burgemeester Honnerlage Gretelaan. *Prof. J. H. van den Broek and Prof. J. B. Bakema, 1956–1957.*

Bakery, Broersvest. *E. F. Groosman, 1959–1960.*

Railway station, platform roofing and platform buildings. *K. van der Gaast and G. J. van der Grinten, 1959.*

## SITTARD

Cultural centre, theatre, cinema, etc. *A. Swinkels and J. H. A. Huysmans, 1957.*

## SPIJKENISSE

Roman Catholic church, Lisstraat. *J. A. Lelieveldt and H. Lap, 1962.*

Shopping centre. *Rein H. Fledderus, 1962–1963.*

## TERNEUZEN

Juliana Hospital, 25a Steenbergenlaan. *J. P. Kloos, 1951–1954.*

Zeeuwsch Vlaanderen Waterworks Company, office building, *J. M. Kuiper, F. J. Gouwetor, J. de Ranitz and R. D. Bleeker, 1955.*

## TIEL

St. Andreas Hospital. *Theo Taen and Dr. Thomas Nix, 1962.*

## TILBURG

Theatre, Markt. *B. Bijvoet and Prof. G. H. M. Holt, 1960.*

Roman Catholic church, Petrus Canisiusstraat. *J. Strik, 1960–1962.*

Catholic School of Economics, Hogeschoollaan. *Jos Bedaux and J. A. van der Laan, 1958–1962.*

Railway station. *K. van der Gaast, 1964 onwards.*

## UITHOORN

International Business Machines laboratory. *D. van Mourik and J. W. du Pon, 1960–1963.*

## UITHUIZERMEEDEN

Houses for the aged. *M. Boom, (the Van Tijen, Boom and Posno work group), 1956.*

## UTRECHT

Nederland-Kattenburg, clothing store, 3 Viestraat. *H. A. Maaskant 1954.*

'Hoograven' houses. *G. T. Rietveld*, 1954–1956.

Juliana Hall, Industries Fair Buildings, Graadt van Roggenweg. *G. T. Rietveld* assisted by *J. A. v. d. Berg, A. J. ter Braak, J. B. van Grunsven and W. Prey*, 1955–1956.

Herderplein shopping centre. *E. F. Groosman* assisted by *P. C. Bos*, 1955.

Professor Kohnstamm School, 1 Marislaan. *D. J. Schenk*, 1955.

Spinoza School, Cervanteslaan, *D. J. Schenk*, 1956.

Houses, Graadt van Roggenweg. *Arthur Staal*, 1956.

Reformed church, Herderplein. *F. C. J. Dingemans*, 1956.

Polymeric N.V., plastics factory, Elektronweg. *H. A. Maaskant*, 1957.

Home for the aged, Dodt van Flensburglaan. *A. Komter*, 1958.

Nederlandse Aluminium Mij. N.V., extension to office building, 1 Groenewoudse Dijk. *H. A. Maaskant*, 1958.

Leefsma N.V., showroom and offices, St. Jacobsstraat. *H. A. Maaskant*, 1958.

'Werkspoor' N.V., factory buildings and office, Utrecht-Zuilen. *Prof. M. F. Duintjer*, 1958–1960.

Group of houses, studios, etc., Burgemeester Norbriuslaan, Utrecht-Zuilen. *Arthur Staal*, 1959.

Mytyl School, Kromme Rijn. *Fons van den Berg*, 1960.

Roman Catholic Church of Christ the King, Marshalllaan. *C. H. Bekink*, 1960.

Offices, Mariaplaats/Rijnkade. *Op Ten Noort-Blijdenstein Bureau*, 1960.

Block of flats, Frederick Hendrikstraat. *P. H. Dingemans*, 1960.

Office building, Industries Fair buildings, Vredenburg. *Prof. P. Elling*, 1960.

House, Breitnerlaan. *G. T. Rietveld*, 1960–1961.

Marijke Hall, Industries Fair Buildings, Graadt van Roggenweg. *Rein H. Fledderus*, 1962.

## VAALS

St. Joseph's Church. *J. H. A. Huysmans*, 1957.

## VALKENBURG

Roman Catholic church, Walramplein. *A. J. N. Boosten*, 1961.

## VELP

Villa. 48 Beekhuizenseweg. *G. T. Rietveld*, 1951.

Grammar School, Ringallee. *R. D. Bleeker*, 1960

## VELSEN

Blast Furnaces office building. *W. M. Dudok*, 1950–1951.

Row of shops, Lange Nieuwestraat. *Prof. J. H. van den Broek and Prof. J. B. Bakema*, 1955.

Ventilation shafts, Velsen Tunnel. *D. Roosenburg*, 1957.

Extension to P.E.N. (Provincial Electricity Network) power station. *Prof. H. T. Zwiers*, 1959.

## VENLO

Railway station, Stationsplein. *K. van der Gaast and W. J. Drees*, 1958.

Factory, Industriestraat. *Prof. G. J. van der Grinten*, 1959.

Dano-installation. *J. W. H. C. Pot and J. F. Pot-Keegstra*, 1959.

Roman Catholic church of St. Nicholas, van Postelstraat. *Prof. G. J. van der Grinten*, 1961.

## VENRAY

Roman Catholic church „Vredeskerk",
Molenplein. *T. H. A. Boosten*, 1964.

## VLAARDINGEN

Houses, Van Hogendorplaan. *E. F. Groosman*,
1952–1954.

Home for the aged, Burgemeester Pruissingel.
*Spruyt and Den Butter's Bureau*, 1953–1955.

House, 94 Prins Bernhardlaan.
*Romke de Vries*, 1954.

'Nieuwe Matex' N.V., Westerlaan 10. *J. W. C.
Boks*, 1955.

Delta Hotel, Maas Boulevard.
*J. W. C. Boks*, 1955.

Vlaardingen Oost railway station.
*K. van der Gaast*, 1956.

Suburban houses, Van Heutsz Park.
*H. P. C. Haan*, 1955.

Gerfa tools factory on the Schiedam-Vlaar-
dingen road. *H. A. Maaskant*, 1956.

Houses, Van Hogendorplaan.
*J. M. Heikens and J. Nuyt*, 1956.

Primary school, Billitonlaan. *W. H. Spruyt
and G. den Butter*, 1956.

Police station, Delftse Veer. *M. F. Duintjer*,
1957.

Houses, Westwijk. *van Tijen, Boom and
Posno*, 1957–1960.

Internationale Rubber Producten N.V., rubber
factory, 11 Mercuriusstraat. *H. A. Maaskant*,
1957.

Rembrandt School, Broekweg.
*Jac. van der Vlis*, 1958.

General Hospital administration building, 8a
Holyweg. *J. W. C. Boks, W. Eykelenboom and
A. Middelhoek*, 1958.

E.N.C.K. recreation centre, Westlandseweg.
*J. van der Vlis and J. van Pelt*, 1959.

E.N.C.K. office building, 21 Parallelweg.
*J. W. C. Boks, W. Eykelenboom and A. Middel-
hoek*, 1959, 1964.

## VOLENDAM

Roman Catholic church, Julianaweg/Kerk-
straat. *H. T. Oudejans and A. C. Alberts*, 1962.

## VOORBURG

Blocks of flats, Nicolaas Beetslaan.
*Romke de Vries*, 1954.

Row of shops and houses, Prins Bernhardlaan.
*W. H. Spruyt and G. den Butter*, 1956.

Church hall of the Netherlands Protestant
Association. *J. J. Hornstra and J. Gerbracht*, 1956.

Fountain Church (Protestant), 1–3 Fonteynen-
buyklaan. *G. W. van Essen*, 1958.

District telephone exchange, Prinses Irenelaan.
*H. A. Maaskant*, 1959.

Prinses Beatrix School for Girls, Van Horvette-
straat. *G. W. van Essen*, 1959.

Protestant Grammar School, Prinses Irenelaan/
Jac. van der Eyndestraat. *Cornelius Elffers*,
1960.

Protestant church, Rembrandtlaan,
*Rein H. Fledderus*, 1964.

## VOORSCHOTEN

Villa, Bachlaan. *Oyevaar, Stolle and Van Gool*,
1960.

Bungalows, Briklaan. *C. J. de Bruin*, 1961.

## VUREN

Villa, Hammel. *Klunder and Witstok*, 1960–1961.

## WAALRE

House. *H. Salomonson*, 1961.

## WAGENINGEN

Agricultural Research Building, Prof. Ritsema

Bosweg. *Van Tijen, Boom and Posno*, 1958–1961.

## WASSENAAR

Grammar School, Backershagenlaan.
*J. P. Kloos*, 1951–1952.

House, 81 Buurtweg. *B. Merkelbach and Prof. P. Elling*, 1954.

De Burcht Flats, 25 Bloemluststraat.
*J. J. Hornstra*, 1958.

Villa, 13 Slingerweg. *A. Fokke van Duyn*, 1957–1958.

Villa, Konijnenlaan, corner of Nachtegaallaan. *A. Fokke van Duyn*, 1958.

Villa, Bloemcamplaan. *A. Fokke van Duyn*, 1958.

Villa, 24 Van Bronckhorstlaan.
*F. U. Verbruggen and P. R. Goldschmidt*, 1958.

Villa, Buurtweg/Dennelaan.
*Prof. P. Elling*, 1960.

Infant school, Verlengde Beukenlaan.
*J. H. W. C. Pot and J. F. Pot-Keegstra*, 1960.

House, Pieter Postlaan/Wassenaarse weg.
*A. Fokke van Duyn*, 1963–1964.

## IJMUIDEN

Houses, Moerbergplantsoen and Gijzeveldplantsoen. *W. van Tijen and H. A. Maaskant*, 1950.

Houses, Lange Nieuwstraat. *Arthur Staal*, 1953.

Bethlehem Church. *J. Schipper*, 1956.

Protestant church near Lange Nieuwstraat.
*K. F. G. Spruyt and A. ten Broek*, 1956.

Block of flats, Moerbergplantsoen.
*Arthur Staal*, 1957.

Block of flats, Maasstraat/Waalstraat.
*Arthur Staal*, 1960.

## ZAANDAM

Verkade's biscuit factory, between Reigerstraat and Westzijde. *A. Eibink*, 1953.

Primary schools, *G. M. G. Bakker*, 1954–1956.

Protestant church, Burgemeester Ter Loonplantsoen/Keplerstraat. *K. L. Sijmons*, 1958.

## ZANDVOORT

Blocks of flats, Boulevard Paulus Loot.
*J. W. H. C. Pot and J. F. Pot-Keegstra*, 1951.

Rotonde Café-Restaurant and adjacent houses.
*A. Komter*, 1954.

'Huis in de Duinen' (House in the Dunes), Home for the Aged. *W. van Tijen and M. Boom*, 1956.

## ZEIST

Protestant Church of St. Thomas, Julianaplein.
*Prof. M. F. Duintjer*. 1962,

## ZEVENAAR

Turmac cigarette factory, Kerkstraat.
*W. S. van de Erve and M. Zwaagstra*, 1947–1949.

Gimborn factory (office requisites).
*H. Geels*, 1958.

Roman Catholic church, Doesburgseweg.
*P. H. A. Starmans*, 1961.

## ZUIDLAREN

Commercial exhibition hall for agricultural products. *G. Th. Rietveld*, 1960.

## ZUTPHEN

Comprehensive Secondary School, Isendoornstraat. *J. A. Kuiper, F. J. Gouwetor, J. de Ranitz and R. D. Bleeker*, 1951.

Railway station, Stationsplein.
*H. G. J. Schelling*, 1952.

Flats, Looiersstraat. *F. Klein*, 1957.

IJsselkade Café. *C. Nielsen*, 1957.

Reesink & Co. N.V., extension to offices and stores, Havenstraat. *H. A. Maaskant and F. Klein*, 1958.

Secondary Agricultural School, 4 Julianalaan. *J. Wiedijk*, 1958.

Protestant church, Wilhelminalaan. *H. Geels*, 1958.

Home for the aged, Coehoornsingel, *J. A. Wentink*, 1958.

Infant school, Isendoornstraat. *D. L. Landman*, 1958.

Houses for the aged, Hoofdgracht. *G. K. Veeze and F. J. Twijnstra*, 1962–1963.

## ZWOLLE

Schrale's Beton en Aannemings Mij. N.V., offices, Willemsvaart. *G. T. Rietveld*, 1958.

Blocks of flats. Buserstraat/Schuurmanstraat. *Ch. van Heelsbergen*, 1958.

Blocks of flats, Hardesteinstraat/ten Oeverstraat. *L. H. O. Buchta and H. G. Treep*, 1959.

Blocks of flats, Pieter Steynstraat. *C. Nap and G. J. P. van Ede*, 1959.

Bus terminal, Stationsplein. *H. Mastenbroek and J. H. de Herder*, 1959.

Provincial Administration Building. *Prof. M. F. Duintjer*, 1964 onwards.

## Photographs by:

Anefo, Amsterdam – N. V. De Arbeiderspers, Amsterdam – R. Blijstra, Amsterdam – Gerrit Burg, Rotterdam – Martien Coppens, Eindhoven – Kees van Dam, Vreeland – C. A. Deul, Hilversum – Bern. van Gils, Breda – Hulskamp's Fotobedrijf, Utrecht – I.B.M. Laboratorium–Photography Dept., Amsterdam – K.L.M. Aerocarto N.V., Schiphol – G. J. Lauwers, Utrecht – Int. Photopress Office, Rotterdam – Nepon, Amsterdam – PublicWorks Dept., Amsterdam – E. M. van Ojen, 's-Gravenhage – Jaap d'Oliviera, Amsterdam – Public Works Dept., Rotterdam – J. L. du Parant, Dordrecht – J. Th. Piek, 's-Gravenhage – Publicam, Amsterdam – H. Sibbelee, Amsterdam – Spies, Amsterdam – W. K. Steffen, De Steeg – Jan Versnel, Amsterdam – J. A. Vrijhof, Rotterdam – Ad Windig, Amsterdam – Het Zuiden, 's-Hertogenbosch – Press and Publicity Dept., Netherlands Postal and Telecommunications Service, 's-Gravenhage.